Women Who Carry
Their Men

Audrey —

Hattie Hill

Enjoy

❏ ❏ ❏

Hattie

Horizon Communications Group Book
ODENWALD PRESS
Dallas

PUBLISHED BY ODENWALD PRESS, DALLAS

Jacket design and illustrations by Graphic Design Group
Conroe, Texas

Library of Congress Cataloging-in-Publication Data

Hill, Hattie, 1958 -
    Women Who Carry Their Men / Hattie Hill
        ISBN: 1-884363-11-3

Printed in the United States of America
10 9 8 7 6 5 4 3 2 1

*This book is dedicated to my mom,
Carrie Flowers,
my sisters, Bernice, Dorothy, Glenda,
Phyllis and Jennifer
and to my niece, Raven,
and the next generation of strong women.*

Foreword

This book is long overdue. I know from personal experience what happens when a woman takes the financial and emotional lead in a relationship. I've been there. Done that. And I bought the T-shirt.

My friend, Hattie Hill, has been there too. Powerful women often have a tough time with relationships. A successful marriage for these women often hinges on striking a balance between fast-paced careers and the demands of any relationship. Most of us were unprepared for the changes success would bring to our lives, but, particularly, to our relationships. As I heard one of my friends say one evening, "All the world's a stage and most of us are desperately unrehearsed."

As I read this book, I was struck by how much I identified with the women who are talking about the frustrations and resentments of carrying. There are so many issues they had to deal with: the surprise of finding themselves the primary provider; the subtle issues of control that take over as their career soars; the high expectations of these women and their willingness to take on most of the responsibility in order to see those expectations fulfilled; the willingness of their husbands and family to let themselves be carried as they, in turn, abdicate responsibilities; and, finally, destruction of the relationships as the women burned out.

I know how many hours of effort and hard work are required to give a first-class performance. But I always assumed that when I fell in love, I'd stay in love, just as I assumed that when I grew up, I'd be grown up. But being in love and growing up takes just as much effort as being elected to the Rock 'n Roll Hall of Fame. I believe in setting goals. Being in the Rock 'n Roll Hall of Fame was one goal the Pips and I set and achieved. Having a good marriage was another goal. And, finally, I have achieved that also, with my friend, lover, and husband, Les Brown. But we had a lot to learn about love and growing up before we achieved that goal.

I was so glad to see the solutions offered by *Women Who Carry Their Men*. While struggling under the weight of carrying someone, it is hard to see solutions. It is not natural for women to dominate any more than it is natural, believe it or not, for men to dominate. We were meant to be helpmates — to work together, to grow together, to play together, and to laugh together.

Gladys Knight

Preface

The idea for this book emerged from my experience in teaching women's programs. I heard over and over the difficulty working women were having reconciling their original expectations of marriage with the challenging new realities of today's two-income families. I kept hearing from successful, career women who were now shouldering a disproportionate share of the load. They were, in effect, carrying their men.

It was a hush-hush issue. The women were embarrassed, and, in most cases, never shared it with their peers or co-workers. They certainly never spoke of it in a group presentation. Only when we had occasion to be alone did they bring it up. Often, women would come up to me after a presentation and say, "Can I speak with you privately?" Each of them thought they were the only person dealing with the confusion and frustration of finding themselves head of the household.

For most, the situation presented difficulties they never expected when they first married. The men resented their wives' success. The wives couldn't understand how they succeeded while the men got left behind. Both parties were unhappy.

After hearing so many stories, I realized we were dealing with a common occurrence that was simply not talked about, in much the same way as women are often too embarrassed (or afraid) to talk about domestic violence in their homes.

Whoa! I thought. Here is something that needs airing — not only to help other women, but also allow us to help ourselves.

I used the word "us," because I am included, too. In the midst of my fast-growing business, my relationship with my husband underwent tremendous changes. I was moving too fast to see those changes. Only after hearing from so many other women did I wake up and realize I had also become a woman who carries. By then, it was too late to save our once-happy relationship. Only after my divorce did I stop long enough to wonder if the outcome might have been different if I had been better informed of the warning signs of carrying a spouse.

This book is not a scientific study. It is a collage of experiences from women across the country. The names of the women are changed and their situations altered to protect their anonymity, but they represent many of us. It is not just the executive woman in the corner office who is carrying the load. It is the woman who helps you deposit your money at the bank, the customer service representative on the phone, the lady who checks your groceries. We are everywhere.

Nor is this book just a woman's gripe session. We are turning the mirror on ourselves to see what role we played. How did we get into this situation? What part did we play? How can we change the situation if we are still married? What can we do differently next time if we are not?

We must do this — take an in-depth look at ourselves — if we want to stop the cycle. Otherwise, we can expect it to occur again and again in an endless spiral.

So, we invite you into our living room for a conversation — with women who carry their men.

Acknowledgments

None of these words would have made it to the page without the encouragement and support of many wonderful people.

I am grateful:

To my family, who shared life experiences with me and helped to shape the person I am today, and to my extended family, to the New Hope Community, and to my friends who allowed me to stretch and grow.

To writer Shirley Schwaller, whose patience and guidance helped bring this book out of my head and onto the page; to Beverly Forté for her editorial and personal excellence; to Sylvia Odenwald for guidance and consultation; to Lyn Sekiguchi for her help in countless details in putting this book together; and to Les Brown, Gladys Knight and Jan Miller for their contribution and encouragement in this project.

To the special women who help to breathe life into this book — thanks for sharing yourself.

To my circle of friends who pushed me constantly, and to my New Years' Eve gang who challenged me to finish this book.

Above all, thanks to the many women around the world who have touched my life. You made a difference. To God be the glory.

Contents

Chapter 1

Women Who Carry Their Men

In a world of two-income families, there is strong anecdotal evidence that not only is June Cleaver of *Leave It To Beaver* fame gone, but she has been replaced by a host of women shouldering a disproportionate share of the family load — financial and emotional. I call it carrying.

Over and over in my speaking and training sessions, both nationally and internationally, women approach me about the stress they are under because they are carrying the lion's share of the responsibility in their relationships and marriages. Of course, carrying the full load is a given for single mothers. It is not a given for married women. Most of these women visualized having a partnership with their husbands when they married.

They visualized a relationship in which each partner supported the other. One might be a step ahead at one point, and another might be two steps ahead at another. On occasion, one or the other might need additional emotional support to weather life's storms. But, basically, they would be sharing the load. That is not what happened.

Instead, these women found themselves way ahead of their husbands, both financially and in other aspects. As their husbands fell behind, they found themselves shoring up their husbands emotionally and taking on increased responsibilities in all aspects of their lives. Before long, often without realizing what was happening, they found themselves shouldering the full weight of the financial and emotional loads. They were carrying.

Webster's dictionary defines carry in its first definition as "to move while supporting, convey, transport." It also defines carry as "to bear the weight or burden." Both definitions fit the situations described in this book. Certainly, these are women who just picked up their spouses and took greater responsibilities rather than slow down their momentum. But, in doing so, they found themselves carrying a bigger burden than they could comfortably bear.

Often, at some turning point, they realized they were exhausted. They couldn't go on. My own story fits the pattern.

HATTIE—ON THE FAST TRACK

I was the fourth of six daughters raised by a single mom in rural Arkansas. We were poor, my mom worked a factory job, and we raised okra to supplement our income. I learned responsibility early. My mom was both father and mother, and she did both admirably. She loved and nurtured us, but she also doled out discipline with a hard hand. "No excuses," was her motto.

If I told her I didn't feel well, she would say, "Go on to school. You'll feel better after awhile." Once I was at school I had no way to get home so, regardless of how I felt, I had to make it through the day.

When we had a flat tire, mom would hop out and change it herself, even if there were three men standing around. My great-grandmother, my aunt, and my cousin were just like her. I came from a family of women who *got things done.*

By the time I was in high school I, too, was taking charge. My biggest desire was to get off the farm. I worked in the field beside our small house and watched the planes fly overhead. "Some day, I'm going where those planes are going," I vowed. That was my dream.

The first step was getting out of our small town. I joined every school organization that took a bus trip to anywhere, just so I could travel.

The second step was education. I knew education was my real ticket to the world outside rural Arkansas. Mom didn't have the money for college, so, in addition to grants and loans for low-income students, I applied for every scholarship that sounded remotely possible from the high school counselor's scholarship listings. I garnered enough money for my freshman year at college to more than pay my way. In fact, I lived better than some of my more affluent friends.

When I graduated with a masters degree in counseling and psychology, I took a job in a small town outside San Diego. There I met my husband.

My sorority sister and I had gone out for a birthday celebration. As I surveyed the dance floor, I spotted the best-looking man, a man in a burgundy jacket twirling a young lady with ease and grace. At the age of 23, I had an eye out for handsome men. So, later that evening when he asked me to dance, I was thrilled. And it only got better. He was an accountant, a professional, and had just joined a company near to my office. I spent the rest of the evening telling him what I knew about life in the area.

We formed a friendship and were soon dating. Older, once married, and wiser than me, my husband-to-be took our relationship slowly. We became friends first. I was dead set on getting to Dallas. That was my goal, and I shared that goal with him. He was an independent person with his own interests and hobbies. So, he didn't push. And our friendship blossomed. By the time a job offer came through in Big D two years later, we were engaged.

He found an accounting position in Dallas a few months later, and we were married. We were buzzing the first few years. We had comfortable jobs, he with a major firm, me with the state. We were partners. We were friends. We had fun — lots of fun.

And then I jumped on the fast track. Bored with my job and needing a challenge, I started a part-time training and consulting business from our home. My husband was very supportive. The first all-day seminar I gave, he called me at noon, and said, "I've been thinking about you all morning. I'm praying for you and with you." He was great! And the seminar went great!

The business took off like a flash, far exceeding either of our expectations. I was soon making money, lots of money. I quit my state job. We bought a bigger house, nicer cars, and I began to accumulate furnishings, and china, and crystal — nice things I did not have growing up.

But my husband was not happy. He felt like he needed to keep up. He began to compete. He wanted to move to New York to get a better job. I became pregnant during this time, but I lost the baby. And after surgery, any thoughts of further children were gone. I would have no more pregnancies. We moved to New York, but I was not happy. I wanted to be back in Dallas where my business contacts were.

Finally, I announced, "I'm going back to Dallas."

And I did. We had a commuter marriage for a year, but my husband, wanting a traditional marriage, finally moved back. It was a case of mismatched expectations.

All my childhood dreams of traveling were being fulfilled. I had business throughout the United States and overseas in South Africa, Europe, and the Caribbean. On most nights, I was not there when my husband came home. He grew increasingly unhappy. And I, finding a tense atmosphere at home, traveled even more.

And I was carrying. My husband spent several months job-hunting after he returned to Dallas. Meanwhile, I bought a large house and paid the bills. I didn't care. It wasn't a problem. I had plenty of money. Because of my fast-paced lifestyle, I was also making quick decisions — lots of them. Pretty soon, I was making all of them.

And I was meeting exciting, new friends. My friends became my husband's friends as we entertained together, but, in the interim, we lost contact with other, older friends from our former life.

My husband and I grew more distant. What I call The Airport Test should have been a clue. When I first started traveling, he would meet me at the gate, give me a big hug, smile, and ask me how the program went. After awhile, he began to pick me up at the curb after I retrieved my luggage. Finally, he suggested I take my own car to the airport.

In a last-ditch effort to compete with my business, my husband started an accounting firm in another city. It wasn't his dream, though. He didn't really want the headaches of administering a business. He was a good accountant, not an entrepreneur. So, he let the business go and returned to Dallas, but he was increasingly frustrated with our life together. He was no longer happy in his work and took to spending the money I earned lavishly and quickly. We were at an impasse.

My genuinely nice, professional husband was also genuinely unhappy. So was I. Finally, after another two years of soul-searching, we split up. Divorce wasn't easy for either of us because of our religious backgrounds. There was no adultery, or violence, or any of the usual, valid reasons for splitting up — just accumulated frustration and exhaustion from our mismatched expectations.

Only in retrospect did I have time to reflect and wonder if the scenario might have played out differently. What role did I play? Why were we not taking turns leading versus my carrying? What might I have done differently? What might we have done differently? What do I need to be aware of before I become romantically involved again? Why was I making all the decisions? Why was I making most of the money? Was it me, him, or us? I never intended to carry. It started in small ways and grew.

I wasn't the only one asking these questions. I heard it from countless other women. That's the genesis of this book. And the purpose.

A small group of us talked through these questions together. This book is our collective observations. As you read, you will meet these women who carried or who are still carrying their men. We found common characteristics among us. And we found common warning signs that the relationship was tilting off balance. We also discovered the cycle of carrying that repeats itself over and over in a downward spiral until we hit the ground and can go no further. But, most important of all, we found some solutions put forth by women who have been there and come out the other side.

Let's begin by meeting seven other women.

MY POINTS OF CONFLICT

These were some of the points of conflict I was experiencing in my marriage.

❏ Different expectations of a marriage
❏ Demands of a fast-paced lifestyle
❏ Growing difference in income
❏ Frequent travel in career
❏ Poor communication
❏ Shift in load of responsibility

What points of conflict are you experiencing in your relationship?

❏
❏
❏
❏

Sue

Joan

Maddie

Maria

Kate

Sarah

Tamara

Chapter 2

Meet Seven More Women Who Carry

SUE—THE HAND OF FATE

Carrying the financial responsibility for our family of five was a conscious decision John and I made together. It was supposed to be a temporary arrangement, but it didn't turn out that way. Instead, ten years later, I am still the primary breadwinner.

When John and I married our senior year of college, we agreed I would stay home after the children were born. Both of our mothers had been full-time homemakers.

At first, our plan was on track. A merchandising/marketing major with artistic talent, John went to work for a Texas interior design company and was soon so much in demand that he formed his own firm in the 1980s. He made good money designing unique and lavish interiors for nouveau rich clients in the heady, quick-money days of high-priced oil and escalating real estate deals in Texas.

I went to work in the sales department of a national frozen food service company. But I kept postponing pregnancy because I liked working and couldn't bring myself to stay home as planned when children arrived. Finally, after eight years of marriage, we decided we could both still work even if we had children. Soon, a son was born and later two daughters.

After the children were born, our tax accountant talked us into building a big house. With John's high earnings, we needed write-offs to lower our tax bill. So, we bought two acres of land and built a large house north of the city. The children were three, five, and seven years old.

Then, the oil bust arrived, depleting a major revenue fuel in Texas' economy. It was followed by the 1986 Tax Reform Act in Congress that eliminated the tax shelter advantages of real estate syndication. The quick decline in real estate prices produced widespread failure in the savings and loan business. Texas was in a depression, and John's business came to a screeching halt. There were no more nouveau rich in Texas — just a bunch of nouveau poor trying to avoid bankruptcy.

The same year I was promoted to director of sales. The promotion meant lots of traveling to different regional offices. I needed to spend more time at work and many days traveling away from home.

So John and I decided he would take over more of the caregiving until the economy (and his interior design clientele) rebounded. He moved his office to our home. Business continued to be slow for John. Meanwhile, the demands of my job grew as the company expanded. With time on his hands, John began to take over all the caregiving — chauffeuring the kids around to their activities, taking them to the doctor and dentist, cooking, grocery shopping.

We had some pretty rough years, financially. Working with one income meant money was tight. We lived in a nice neighborhood, but our large home was like a money pit. Maintenance and repairs ate our lunch. But selling didn't seem wise, either. Our mortgage was more than we could recoup in a down market. So, feeling the financial pressure, I just kept working harder and harder.

At some point, we crossed a threshold where he felt that he couldn't attend to his business because I was relying on him so much to be the caregiver. "How can I get a normal job?" he would ask.

But then that male ego creeps in. He is embarrassed that his wife is the chief breadwinner. He hates it.

In the meantime, I am resentful and frustrated, too. I don't want the whole burden financially. I worry that I'm missing my children's lives and soon they will be gone. We don't know what to do. Our 25-year-old marriage is on rocky ground. We ended up here not by design, but by timing and circumstance.

JOAN—CARRIER FROM DAY ONE

I knew when I married Allen that I would carry the main load financially. I was 37 and a single mom. After my divorce at age 30, I was frightened that we would be poor. I had been a full-time homemaker. But I discovered I had a talent for working with people and established myself as a public relations specialist in a major city. Now, at age 37, I was comfortable that I could support my family.

But finding someone to fill the gap left by divorce was not proving easy. When Allen came along, I found a companion in a sweet man who shared my love of family and home. Allen also was working in public relations, so we shared a common profession as well. When we married, I rationalized the whole marriage to be based on me as the controlling person. He was so innocent and so pure. I loved those qualities. And I thought I could just continue to support myself and my children.

I knew my ambitions and goals for our family were greater than Allen's expectations. He was younger, had never been married, and, I felt, did not realize how much money it took to support a family. From the first day of marriage, I took the lead. I accepted a job in another city that moved me into a management position and doubled my income. Allen followed, but over the course of several years, never found comparable employment.

Early in our new marriage, we had a baby, a third child for me, a first for Allen. Allen adored his small son. There was never any doubt in either of our thoughts that we belonged together as a family.

But my initial intention to be the main breadwinner was proving a harder burden than I had envisioned. Although, I was by now head of public relations at a large advertising agency, I felt pressure to earn more money with our older children approaching college age. I started my own public relations company, thinking this was the way to build wealth. It proved to be hard. Shortly after starting the company, the bottom fell out of the economy. Companies were failing in the depressed market. We held on, but only by my working longer and longer hours. We forged an alliance with a major corporation to infuse money into the company and expand its capabilities into the national advertising arena. Then, the corporation was bought out by another company and the deal fell through. After seven years of intensely hard work, I was exhausted. I sold the company on a future promise of money if the new owner did well and went home, too tired to even think of job hunting.

After the sale, Allen, who by this time had joined the company to help in the proposed expansion, was jobless, too.

"It's up to you," I told him. I was too tired to carry the financial load further. My initial intention to carry the family financially was proving too tough.

MADDIE—THE DIALYSIS PATIENT

At twenty, I lost both my kidneys. That was 1974. Except for a brief period in the 1980s when I had a kidney transplant that ultimately failed, I have had to hook up to a dialysis machine six hours a night, three times a week, to clean my blood.

I was popular in high school. I was little and cute and had several guys asking me out when I developed kidney problems and became very ill. At one point, I even lost my eyesight, but, by the grace of God and through the prayers of my church family, my eyesight was restored. My life centered around church and school in the small town where I was raised. My mother and father were divorced and my father moved away, so I was raised by my mom and grandmother. They were strong women. They taught me to pray, to respect my elders, and to be responsible.

I fell passionately in love while I was in college with a guy I knew from my hometown. He joined the service after high school, but we wrote letters and saw each other occasionally. I tasted passion with him.

When I became ill again and lost my kidneys, I lost my boyfriend at the same time. He was stationed in Germany when I last heard from him. There was no official break up. We simply stopped writing. I guess we both understood that he couldn't deal with a woman who was permanently hooked up to a dialysis machine.

I carried the memory of that first passion with me and thought I would never experience that kind of love again. Dialysis changes your appearance. I was rail thin and weak. My hair fell out. My skin turned dark and ashen. It looked like tar.

Then I met Lionel at church. "How are you doing, Miss Lady," he said. I was thrilled to have a handsome, sophisticated man call me "Miss Lady." He made me feel pretty again.

We began to go out with a group, and Lionel was always very tender with me. He was the lead singer in a local band and had lots of lady friends. I knew that, but I was pleased to be his friend. As a work- and church-centered girl, it was an adventure to go to the clubs with him. And I felt safe with Lionel. He always looked out for me.

Lionel began to ask me why I always wore long sleeves and wigs, so I told him about the dialysis. I wore long sleeves to cover up the bandaged bumps caused by the needles that pierced my skin three times a week.

"So, what," he said. "You're a good-looking woman. A few bandages don't matter."

I began to wear shorter skirts and short-sleeved blouses. He got me to quit wearing wigs that covered up my stubby hair left from treatment. Instead, I styled my short locks in a bob that stuck close to my head. It looked almost stylish in an avant garde way. He encouraged me to grow my nails long, which I did. I polished them to a fine shine with bright nail polish. I began to feel pretty. I loved all the attention.

My worldly and street-wise friend, Lionel, also dated other women. But, over time, we became more than friends. We became lovers. Lionel reawakened a sexual urge I had lost.

When he proposed marriage, I said no. I told him he didn't understand my life, really. The dialysis machine is not a pretty picture. So he spent nights with me while I went through treatments and drove me home afterwards. I made sure he understood about dialysis. I told him I would always be sick, off and on. I might lose my job because of my disability. I couldn't have children.

Still, he stayed. By now we were living together, an arrangement my mother was very much against. But I needed someone and I loved him so much.

Finally, I told him I wanted to get married. I was always taught marriage is forever and didn't want to chance a divorce. I told Lionel that if he wanted someone else, I would step aside. I was used to being put aside by then. I felt I could always go back to my world of church, work, and home.

Lionel told me he had to clean up some relationships before he could commit to me. He never lied about that.

When we married, we moved into my apartment. I had the stuff — furniture, television, stereo, dishes. Lionel was a musician and worked construction when he needed money. But after awhile, he quit the construction. By the time we were married three years, I was pretty much the financial support. The money from his gigs went into his pocket, not to pay our bills. But the stress of carrying all the financial responsibility was hurting my health. Dialysis makes you fight for life, and it is a tough fight. Additional stresses can pull you down pretty quick.

I couldn't handle it. I told Lionel to get a job or leave.

He did get a job at a factory. And for awhile, we were happy. We were sharing bills and things were fine.

But it wasn't to last forever. The next crisis would really stretch our ability to survive as husband and wife.

MARIA—THE PARENT

I grew up in a large family, six brothers and sisters. I assumed that, after graduation from high school, I would marry and have a large family, too. But my high school sweetheart and I split up shortly before graduation. So, I went to live with a cousin in a large city and found work as a secretary.

I did marry, eventually, when I was twenty-five, but the marriage lasted less than a year. My first husband got hooked on drugs and, sensing disaster, I walked. I always felt guilty about walking out so quickly on that marriage.

I was 33 before I married again. By that time, I had been working fifteen years and was in management at a large company. I made good money, more money than I ever expected to earn.

When I met Joe, he was working at a health club. He was the happiest, most carefree person I ever met. He didn't have a care in the world. He lived off cash, whatever he earned. I loved his enthusiasm for life, but most of all I loved that he accepted me just as I was. He didn't try to change me or tell me what to do. He just let me be me. We fell in love, and we got married.

The first year of our marriage was hell. All the issues we hadn't dealt with before marriage came stomping into our lives.

Because Joe lived off cash, he had no credit. I had bought a nice house in the suburbs outside the city. That was OK. But after marriage, I wanted him to help with the house payments. That was a problem. He never had enough cash to take on that large a payment.

He decided to start a plumbing business with a buddy. Before we married, Joe had a very successful plumbing business. He made more than $100,000 a year, but he spent every dime. When he tired of working so hard, he left the business and went to work at the health club. When we married, he didn't have a pot to pee in.

So, he thought he could duplicate that success with a new plumbing business. His buddy, however, turned out to be a crook. I had been in the business world a long time, and I saw the red flags. When his partner kept coming up with reasons why they weren't being paid on time, I kept telling Joe something was wrong. But Joe, who is completely trusting, kept telling me I didn't understand his business. We fought over his inaction. Finally, I convinced Joe to check the account at the bank. Begrudgingly, he did. The account had been closed and a new account opened under his partner's name to which Joe had no access. His partner spent the money as soon as it came in the door. Joe was left with nothing.

So, during the first year of our marriage, I was paying all the bills.

We both wanted a family. During that first year, we found out pregnancy was going to be a problem. We went to a fertility doctor and were soon taking a clinical approach to sex. Lying in bed with a thermometer in your mouth doesn't do much for spontaneity in a physical relationship. That posed an added stress to the financial situation the first year. As Joe says, "I had an affair with Dixie (cup) for a year."

And we were audited by the IRS. After we filed our first joint tax return, the red flags went up all over the IRS computer system. Joe had not filed in five years. By the time they got through with us, we owed them a chunk of change.

"OK," I told Joe. "You are now married to me. I am this beautiful package with bows and glitter. I pay my bills. I am successful at what I do. And I am not going to be brought down by someone who has been totally irresponsible and doesn't give a rats potootie about anything. You affect me — my credibility."

The second year of marriage began better. Joe continued in business on his own, and, by the end of the year, I was pregnant. But Joe's carefree attitude that I found so attractive when I met him was now looking more like total irresponsibility to me. I soon became the parent, constantly instructing him on how to operate a business successfully.

He would get a project and do two-thirds of it, but never finish the details. This behavior does not make for happy, return customers, I told him. Or he would take on three projects at once, rather than one at time, and not finish any completely. For example, he told one couple he would install new pipes inside and outside their home. It was January when he took the job, which is not a good time to be doing any outside work. But he didn't call them and tell them *when* he planned to do the job. I told him more than once to call and talk to them.

"Joe," I said. "Call them. Don't tell someone you will be there and then just not show up without at least calling them. That's common courtesy."

Well, he finally did call — after he got a letter from a lawyer threatening to sue for breach of contract.

We have another lawsuit on our hands, now. Before we were married, Joe was the middle car in an accident. He remembers being hit from behind and then hitting the car in front. I suggested at the time that he take pictures of the car and see a doctor. But he said everything was fine. Well, the statute of limitations for suit was almost up, and in comes this lawsuit alleging Joe hit the car in front of him first before he was hit. Now, it is just his word against this other person's.

I guess his happy-go-lucky attitude delays his involvement until after the fact, rather than propelling him to act. He is reactive, rather than proactive. So much of what he does is crisis intervention.

I have a real need for security and stability. It drives me crazy. I know the situation has to change, particularly now that the baby is here. Our son is three months old. You know, everyone tells you how much you are going to love your baby. And you say, yeah, of course. But I still was not prepared for the emotions I have gone through with this small infant. I really want to stay home and be a full-time mother.

When I told Joe, he looked at me (and I could tell he really hated having to say this) and said, "Maria, I'm just not earning enough for you to do that right now."

His attitude is changing. He realizes he has to step up to the plate and take on more responsibility. He really wants this marriage to work. He really wants to live in a nice house. He really wants to be here with me and the baby. So, we're working at it. It isn't easy, but, for the first time, he is really working hard at it.

KATE—STRONG AND COMPETENT

Richard and I were married nine years. Most of those nine years Richard was, well, missing in action. I should have recognized a red flag when he showed up at our wedding without the ring. Richard was just not there, emotionally or physically. From day one, he abdicated responsibility to me.

I was a junior in college and Richard a senior when we married. After working for a year, we returned to school — me working full time and going to school part-time, Richard working part-time and finishing school on a full-time basis. He planned to be a CPA and I planned to teach high school math.

I knew from the time we dated that he was not financially responsible. He would bounce checks frequently, not because he didn't know how to balance a checkbook, but because he didn't take the time to attend to it. So, I took over the household budget right after we were married, and Richard was glad to hand over the job.

After graduation he earned a good living, but he did not attend to other responsibilities. Over the years, one by one, I found myself managing the entire household and making all the decisions without Richard's input. The weight of the load grew with time, and, with each new crisis, grew heavier and heavier. It also seemed that as he passed off each responsibility, he pulled further away emotionally. So during the tough times, he wasn't there for me. And tough times came.

One was the stress of years of infertility. Emotionally, Richard took his infertility personally and withdrew even further from me. Eventually, we ended up going to an infertility doctor and saw a marriage counselor. During that time, we made some progress and I became pregnant. Our only daughter, a miracle baby, brought us closer for a short time.

Then, I was in an automobile accident and Richard had to take over most of the household responsibilities for a few months. But it proved to be too much for Richard and things just didn't get done.

As soon as I was back on my feet, I again plunged into taking on more and more of the responsibility for maintaining the home. But, by then, I was on maximum overload.

I realized I couldn't go on at the same pace. I was working full time as a teacher, tutoring after work, and trying to care for our daughter. I announced to Richard that I was going to quit my main teaching job. Then, Richard announced he was leaving.

What little safety net I had, dropped away. We had been on parallel paths, and we hadn't connected emotionally in a long time. But I couldn't return to work in an urban school system. I was too burned out. What to do next . . .

After the divorce, I took an independent path, increasing my private tutoring business and enrolling in graduate school. It took years but I didn't quit until I got my doctorate, ultimately becoming a university professor. I realized I could go it alone.

SARAH—DIVERGING PATHS

Marvin and I were married right out of high school. He was my first love. After two years of togetherness as high school sweethearts we married, but our paths quickly diverged. The year was 1974. Marvin was drafted shortly after receiving his high school diploma and sent to Vietnam. Not long thereafter, I discovered I was pregnant. We spent our first year of marriage apart — Marvin in a war zone, me living with my parents in Kansas City. By the time Marvin returned from his twelve-month tour, we had both changed. Marvin was a veteran of one of America's most divisive and bloody wars. I was a mother. Our daughter, Diane, was born two months before Marvin's return.

The Army moved us to California. Partially because I liked the new-found independence I had discovered while living apart and partially because Marvin constantly complained about how tough life was, I went to work. His complaining made me feel guilty for not contributing financially. I started baby-sitting in a nursery and took Diane along. My original goals were to be a full-time homemaker and stay-at-home mom. I envisioned five kids running around our house. But by the age of 22, I was beginning to realize that Marvin didn't want the full financial responsibility. I began to think in terms of how I might earn more.

I found a job as a secretary with the local Chamber of Commerce in the Georgia city where we were now stationed. I also took college courses. Marvin worked nights as an Army mechanic, and we alternated child care. We seldom saw each other. Meanwhile, I was being promoted, first to coordinator for meetings, then as supervisor.

As things evolved, I was also making all the family decisions. That started in the second year of the marriage. Then I took on the responsibility for making those decisions work. By the time we were married ten years, I was running the show.

Two important events converged in 1977. A young computer company offered me a job in their training department. And the Army wanted Marvin to do a three-year tour of duty in Germany. If the family didn't go with him, the Army would reduce the tour to two years.

"I'm not going," I told him after some long thought. "You make your own decision about what's best for you. We'll be here when you return."

Marvin elected to leave the Army. Now, I was really in the lead. Up to now, our incomes had been about equal. My subsequent promotion took us to a new city. Marvin worked as a mechanic, but he wasn't happy. He hated the new city and the people. A car accident put him in rehabilitation for two years. I continued to progress at work, eventually becoming a senior vice president. I was also the sole breadwinner.

Over the next ten years of our marriage, that would prove our undoing.

TAMARA—ACCEPTING MORE AND MORE RESPONSIBILITIES

Phil and I are happily married. But our success is the result of many changes on both our parts. We had to learn how to forge a successful relationship together. It hasn't been easy. "Marriage is like farming," Phil now says. "Everyday you get up and start all over again."

I was devastated when my first husband left me and our three small children. But I pulled myself together, found a job in an insurance agency, sold the home I could not afford to maintain on my own, moved into an apartment, and got on with life.

One day I was jogging at the high school track next door to where the children were in child care. Phil jogged up beside me. I talked to Phil but turned him down when he asked me out. I wasn't interested.

A year later, Phil saw my daughter at the high school and recognized Susie as my child by her eyes. "You are Tamara's daughter?" he asked. Getting an affirmative answer, he found me coaching my son's basketball team in the gym. This time, he invited me to a reading from his recently completed play. Curious, I went to the reading.

It was his creative writing that touched my heart. Coming from my first marriage to a man who couldn't express his feelings, it was very important to me to find a man who could. I wanted a man who could own his feelings.

We started to date. We both recognized immediately that something spiritual and higher than the two of us was happening. We spent hours reading the Bible on dates, something I had never done in my life, much less with a man. We talked often about the fact that there was some other purpose in our coming together. We were just instruments.

I also knew Phil was not a good candidate for a support system for me and the kids. He had a history of job hopping. We married anyway.

The honeymoon didn't last long. Within a week after the wedding, Phil was fired from his position as a tennis coach. He had owned businesses before, a small advertising agency, and an auto parts store. Now, he encouraged me to go to a commercial art institute to develop my natural artistic talents. He, in turn, would start an advertising agency. The idea appealed to me.

Soon, I found myself living a tough schedule. Up at 5 a.m., I worked part-time at the bank to bring in income, went to art school in the afternoon, and returned home to care for the children in the early evening. About 9 p.m., I would start my homework, plus do advertising layouts for Phil's new business. Bedtime didn't come until after midnight.

To complicate matters, Phil's mother asked to live with us. She was near destitute and we had just rented a nice home with four bedrooms. We had the space. How could we say no? But Phil's mom is an alcoholic. Her frequent bouts of depression and anger caused emotional upheavals among all of us — Phil, myself, the children. Within the year, we realized this arrangement was not going to work. Phil called his mother's sister and talked her into taking his mother in.

But I persevered. I had a strong need to be loved. I needed someone there. I had a lot of responsibility growing up, and I felt needed but not loved. My mom was a good worker, but her self-esteem wasn't good. My father was absent a lot, and she just did her job. She didn't show love in demonstrative ways. I was the same way. I worked to get done whatever needed to be done without complaint because of the fear that, if I expected more, my husband might leave.

Within two years, life began to improve for a short time. I graduated and went to work full time in our advertising business. Phil, dynamic and personable, made friends easily. He was invited to join several non-profit boards, gaining a foothold in the community and bringing in business. But over the next four years, everything disintegrated.

Phil was unhappy. He really wanted to devote his time to creative writing. He began to sleep late, not showing up at the office until 11 a.m., then going to lunch and playing tennis in the afternoon. I began to resent the fact that I was at the office early and doing most of the work.

Then, Phil disappeared from the business altogether — watching movies at night and sleeping during the day. He was supposed to be handling the family budget. But, as creditors began to call, I realized nothing was being paid. House payments were behind, the office rent was in arrears, other bills were overdue.

I was really angry and found it hard to talk to him. When I did try to talk with Phil, he would get angry. So I shut down emotionally from him.

Then came an important insight. I realized I couldn't change him or anybody for that matter. A feeling of total hopelessness set in. On that realization, I made some decisions. I separated myself from the advertising agency and started my own graphic design firm. Phil and the agency ended up in bankruptcy court. And I left him. Our home was repossessed, and I moved myself and the children into a small rent house and worked from there. Phil called, but I had nothing to say. He threw away what we had built. I was too hurt and too angry to talk.

It took a Christmas miracle to bring us back together.

HIGH STANDARDS/STRONG NEEDS

These seven women set high standards for themselves and others. They wanted:

- ❏ Control to make things right
- ❏ Perfection in how things are accomplished
- ❏ Completion of tasks within their time frame
- ❏ Order in their lives
- ❏ Financial security
- ❏ Success

They also had a strong need to:

- ❏ Love
- ❏ Be loved
- ❏ Feel valued
- ❏ Feel respected
- ❏ Fulfill commitments

What standards have you set for yourself?

- ☐
- ☐
- ☐
- ☐
- ☐

What are your strong needs?

- ☐
- ☐
- ☐
- ☐
- ☐

Chapter 3

Personal Characteristics Of Women Who Carry

What about us makes us carry? The women we talked with cited a number of characteristics that played a role. A song from the 1950s sums it up pretty well. The chorus started: "Anything you can do I can do better."

All of the women were strong, competent women. And, quite frankly, they had high expectations of themselves and others. Whenever their husbands dropped the ball on an issue or event, these women just picked it up and ran it down the field for a touchdown. They are what I call Low-Maintenance Women.

So am I. As I said to my husband shortly after our marriage, "You told me you loved me when we got married. I won't ask you again. If anything changes, let me know." I didn't expect to be constantly coddled. Life was to be gotten on with. And I was ready to go.

Over time and often very subtly that competence turns into control. When we carry, we also control because we find ourselves making decisions on everything from what car to buy to what school our children attend and what we eat for dinner. In many cases, it's control by abdication from our spouse, but with only one person at the helm, the balance of the relationship is destroyed.

Let me give some examples of these characteristics.

TENDENCY TO TAKE CONTROL

HATTIE. I *hate* the feeling of my being out of control. It disorients me. I become physically ill. Because of my extensive travel and my work with clients, there is a great deal I don't have control over. So in my home life, I feel the need to have a schedule and control.

I can think of a perfect example of wanting to control and how it made me go nuts. In my marriage, I booked all the travel arrangements. It made sense. I was traveling a lot with my business and knew good agents. I earned the frequent flyer miles that made it possible to go to exotic locales. Planning the vacations became one more responsibility on my list. I guess I thought if I didn't do it, we wouldn't go anywhere.

At one point, my husband and I were working in two different cities; I was in Dallas, my husband was on a multi-month assignment in New York. So, I planned a very romantic vacation for the two of us to an isolated island off Tahiti. I set the dates, told my husband what they were, and booked the flights, the hotel, and the rental car. All my husband had to do was show up. In my mind, I had this whole vacation planned out.

We met in San Francisco and caught a flight to our island retreat. The second morning after a leisurely breakfast on the patio (which I suggested), I said, "Let's go for a walk on the beach."

"Great," my husband says.

Well, my idea of walking on the beach is rolling up our pants, strolling at the water's edge, and holding hands. You know? I've seen that on TV, right?

Well, my husband, of course, being an accountant, thinks, let's get on our walking gear. He's out there power walking. I'm like, "Hey, we're not doing that! Let's walk and hold hands."

The net result was a miserable walk. That was only the beginning. We got into a huge argument — then and on the flight back. All I could think of was, how many thousands of dollars did I just waste? I realized the marriage was not working, but I didn't realize what I was doing. I wanted to control every segment of that vacation — from booking the ticket to getting on the airplane right down to how we would look longingly at each other as we walked on the beach.

 MADDIE. I learned control early. My mother and grandmother raised me, and they ran the household. I admired that. And I patterned myself after them. I pretty much raised my younger brother and sister, because my mom held down two jobs. So, when I married, I came with that attitude. I was happy to pay the bills and take care of everything financially. I thought it was up to me to see that nothing collapsed. When something went wrong, Lionel always came to me. And I would take on the job of finding a solution or paying the shortfall he had incurred. For me, it was natural.

Most of us didn't plan to be controlling women. Many women who carry thought they would stay home and take care of a growing family, married to a strong man. Often, control sneaks up. When our husbands drop the ball, we just pick it up and add that item to our to-do list.

 KATE. Richard and I dated from high school into college. While in college, his parents set him up with an account at their bank. If he overdrew, the bank just took money from his parents account to cover the overdraft. So, Richard never had to be accountable for a budget.

I knew Richard was irresponsible about the money, so after we married, I kept the checkbook and paid the bills. We both had good incomes and I tried to involve him in financial decisions, but he didn't care to participate. His consuming interest was in restoring antique cars. The more I did to manage the household, the more time he could spend at the shop. Little by little, and quite unintentionally, he became less and less available and I cut him out of the loop. Before long, I had complete decision-making control. Nobody planned it. It happened through Richard's abdication of all the mundane tasks and my picking up the slack to see that those tasks got done.

 SUE. The original idea was that I would stay home when the children were born. Neither John's mother or mine had worked when we were growing up. Then I discovered I loved working. I loved the success I was experiencing. I worked for a fun-loving company with great employees and I didn't want to quit. So, after eight years of marriage, we changed our idyllic little game plan. We decided I could work *and* have children.

We had three babies in quick succession. Then, John's business went belly up when economic conditions became depressed. At the same time, my career took off. The family was suddenly dependent on me financially.

But it was other characteristics that led to my financial control. John's free-spirited nature was adverse to basic bookkeeping. At one point, I asked him to keep the family checkbook. He totally screwed it up. We had checks bouncing everywhere. After one month, I fired him. It was these kinds of episodes that led to my finally realizing I had taken over.

Before many years passed, everything was in my name. I didn't realize what a hard pill this was for John to swallow until recently. We were paying an annual fee for an American Express Gold card.

I said, "We don't need to pay this charge. Why don't you cancel it?"

But John adamantly refused to cancel it. I was thinking that it was a status symbol he didn't want to discard. But it wasn't that. Finally, one day he said to me when I brought up the subject again, "This is the only credit card we have in *my* name!"

I didn't think about that. All of the cars and credit cards are in my name. When did that happen, I wonder now.

ATTEMPT TO FIX WHATEVER IS WRONG

How many of us at times have longed to crawl into mom's lap, so she can kiss the hurt and make it go away? When we were little, our moms watched out for us, made sure we ate a good breakfast, warned us about strangers, nagged us into doing our homework, and, in my home, doled out discipline liberally if we broke the rules. She had *control*. Those of us blessed with strong, loving mothers looked to her for comfort and guidance. We depended on mom to keep stability and order in our young lives and come to our rescue when we were in trouble.

These characteristics are necessary to give their young children a sense of security growing up. They can have dramatically different results in an adult relationship.

Sarah found that out the hard way.

 SARAH. For twenty-five years, I kept trying to make life easier for Marvin. Every time Marvin complained about how hard or unfair life was, I would step in to make everything better. Marvin's foray into entrepreneurship is a classic example. Marvin, a mechanic during much of his working life, decided he wanted his own business. He wanted to be a real estate appraiser.

"Okay, do that," I encouraged.

Well, the excuses started. "I don't have the right certification," he explained.

"I really can't compete with all the regional and national firms . . . ."

True to form, I began to "fix" the objections. I called a well-known real estate school and applied to get Marvin certified. I also paid the fees. I helped him study for his certification test. I did everything but take the darn test for him.

After Marvin became certified, I called my friends and recruited several as clients for Marvin. I kept thinking that if Marvin were happy, then we would be happy.

But Marvin wasn't happy. He quickly needed more clients, and he looked to me to bring in more business. I was working full time and carrying the household responsibilities. I couldn't be Marvin's full-time prospector. But I didn't quit offering solutions. I suggested he hire someone on a commission basis to find clients.

Instead, Marvin quit the business. Marvin was dependent on my nurturing help. He just couldn't go it alone. In Marvin's mind, it became my fault the business failed, because I wouldn't help him enough. He depended on me to control the process.

COMMITTED TO THE RELATIONSHIP

Commitment is a positive force. Certainly, no relationship, even the best kind in which equal partners are working toward a common goal, can exist for long without commitment. Commitment, along with perseverance, gets us through the rough spots. And the women who carry are committed to their marriage. That commitment has much to do with why we keep on taking on more responsibilities. We want the relationship to work — but we also want it to work on our terms.

 SARAH. My middle name is commitment. I never got married thinking we might someday get divorced. I was absolutely committed to my marriage. I learned early that I could also have my way. Marvin handed off decisions to me right and left. And I was stronger than Marvin. Our biggest fights were over child rearing. Our daughter was born ten months after our wedding. We never even had a conversation about child rearing before she was born. Marvin was overseas in Vietnam during my pregnancy. It didn't take long to realize we had different ideas about child-rearing.

Marvin believed in strong discipline and control — the old "do it because I said so" school of parenting. He wanted to set rules without explanation and have them obeyed.

I believed every situation was at least negotiable. I wanted our daughter to make many of her own decisions within the constraints of basic safety and then learn from the consequences of those decisions. So, Marvin and I fought over everything — who I would let her play with versus who Marvin wanted her to play with; what I would let her eat versus what Marvin thought she should eat; what time I would let her come home versus what time Marvin thought she should be home. We fought so much that I decided we shouldn't have any more children.

It is probably an important point that I almost always won the argument. I was very sure I was right. This had a lot to do with our problems, but it never impacted my commitment to the marriage. That never wavered.

BEING A LOW-MAINTENANCE WOMAN

An important characteristic of all the women who carry is their independence. They are not women who demand much from their men. If the men don't measure up to their expectations, they don't pack their bags and go home to mama. They literally carry on.

I got a strong sense of this possibility as I was helping out a friend, acting as mother confessor to her son, Timmy. Timmy and his wife, Patty, had a huge fight, and my friend asked me if I would go over and see what was going on. She had tried to call, but the phone was unplugged, and the last time she talked to her daughter-in-law, she was in tears.

So, I went over. Timmy was there and I invited him to my house. He came. We're sitting on the sofa talking and I ask him what was wrong.

"Well, when I met her, when I married her, she used to do everything," he replied. "Now, she wants *me* to do all kinds of stuff."

I couldn't believe my ears! "Why do you think she married you?" I asked. "If she is going to do everything, she might as well have stayed by herself."

We drove to their house and I was sitting between the two of them, wondering how I got in this situation again. Before they married, Patty was handling life as a single mom with two small children. She was also nursing her dying mom. Her mother is now dead, but there is another child, a daughter. The baby is now over a year old and toddling around the house, getting into the usual scrapes of the very young and very innocent.

But Timmy was serious. He turned to Patty and said plaintively, "You used to be so strong, and now you want me to help."

"I *was* strong," Patty replied. "I had to be. My mom was sick, and I had two kids to look after. But now I want a partner."

I'm afraid this story does not have a happy ending. Patty's plea went right over Timmy's head. He moved out and got his own apartment using some money he got after his grandmother died. That money was gone in less than a month. He worked a construction job that a friend found for him for three days, then quit.

His wife is now on the verge of homelessness. But she told me recently, "I'm a survivor. I will do whatever it is that I need to do to feed these children and put a roof over their heads." I believe her. And I also believe that is why Timmy was attracted to her. She didn't ask for much. She was a low-maintenance woman.

THE CHARACTERISTICS OF CARRYING

These are some of the characteristics of carrying.

- ❑ High expectations of yourself and others
- ❑ Being a low-maintenance woman
- ❑ Independent
- ❑ Tendency to take control
- ❑ Attempt to fix whatever is wrong
- ❑ Committed to the relationship
- ❑ Perfectionist

Chapter 4

The Signs You Are Carrying

Every marriage, like every relationship, has give and take. At times, you may be experiencing an emotional crisis and need a strong shoulder to hold onto. At other times, your husband may need the support. That's normal. That's natural. Carrying, on the other hand, is a one-way street.

The women I talked to looked back and identified warning signals from their own lives that should have alerted them their relationship was critically unbalanced.

These examples are clear signs that you are carrying someone.

I Am The Parent, You Are The Child

Parents monitor their children. Did you do your homework? Is your room clean? When will you be home? Whose house is the party at? Will their parents be there?

Women who carry, monitor their husbands.

 JOAN. Even though I knew I would be the main financial support when I married Allen, I was unprepared for his procrastination tendencies. I became a nag, really. I would ask Allen to do something, for example, figure out why the hub caps on the car were rattling.

"It's because they need to be tightened," he would reply. That job required taking off the wheels and tightening the hub caps.

"Would you do that?" I might ask.

"Sure," he would reply. But he didn't really mean it. Weeks came and went by. And the car would still rattle.

I would find myself asking constantly. "Are you going to tighten the hub caps?"

"Yes," he would reply. Before long, whenever he told me he would do something, I didn't really believe him. So, I would keep monitoring, asking if the job had been done.

 MARIA. I *am* the parent. My husband has his own plumbing business, but he doesn't really understand some basic business transactions that I consider part of any business. I find myself telling him what to do, when to do it, how to handle situations. At times, I have gotten really rough — the kind of tough love that a

parent might dole out to a child headed down the wrong track.

Joe works on projects. And, at times, he is between projects generated on his own. Once, his buddy asked Joe to work with him on a particular project. Joe did, spending his own money for supplies. Well, the guy didn't pay Joe.

"OK," I said, "you've learned a lesson. Don't ever work for him again."

Well, when the money got low, this guy hit the picture again. He offered Joe a job and promised to pay. Joe, always trusting, took the job. It was the same scenario. Joe spent money for supplies and the guy didn't pay him. Again.

"If you work for this guy again," I told Joe, "I'm gone. That is how serious I am about this."

THE MONEY IS MINE . . . ALL MINE, UNFORTUNATELY

Women who are the principal breadwinner find themselves carrying the responsibilities of buying the house, the car and the groceries, often making the decisions on how the left over money is spent. Most of them did not start their marriages thinking this is what would happen. Like Kate, it happened over time. For some, such as Maddie, the relationship began that way.

KATE. Well, I knew when we married that Richard wasn't responsible with a checkbook and that I would handle that part of our finances. But I still thought our marriage would be more of a partnership than it was. I gradually began to make all of the financial decisions.

At first, I expected him to take care of various responsibilities. I often found that what I thought he was going to do, he hadn't done at all. For example, on one occasion, he volunteered to drop a check I had written for our electric bill in the payment window at the electric company near where he worked. "This is great," I beamed, thinking he was assuming more responsibility. It seemed a simple enough task. But he forgot. He never took the envelope out of his shirt pocket. I didn't realize there was a problem until I got a notice from the electric company threatening to cut off our services. So, I began monitoring things.

When nothing happened, I quit asking him to do even simple things. I just began to do it myself. It was easier. In a way, it was a self-preservation move on my part. I saved myself the stress of having to monitor him and be disappointed.

So, Richard was no longer actively helping. But then he began not wanting to even participate in the decision-making process. He didn't want to be involved at all in buying the house, or buying the car, or picking out furniture. At first, I would ask him what he thought or ask him to go along to look at something I was considering purchasing. But he would turn me down. "Whatever you decide is fine," he said. Finally, I just went and bought whatever we needed without mentioning it to him.

It made life easier for me. He was easy to please. He never complained about my choices. He just didn't want to be involved.

 MADDIE. I controlled the money from the start of our marriage. I had a house. I bought the cars. I paid the bills. Lionel worked only sporadically — construction jobs. In that way, he was free to play with his band when the opportunity arose. Most of his money went to maintaining his image. Lionel always needed three hundred dollars in his pocket, while twenty bucks of pocket change was enough for me. But Lionel felt that when the time came to buy drinks he should be able to roll out a big wad of bills. To him, that was success. He dressed well, too — expensive, two-toned leather shoes, hats, double breasted suits, colored shirts and ties that changed with the seasons.

I wanted him to take more monetary responsibility. At one point, I goaded him into taking a full-time position at a food company. But when the band began to get air time on the local radio station and the number of bookings picked up, he quit again.

So, I continued to pay the bills and the mortgage. I also kept a savings account that he knew nothing about. That was my safety valve in case I got sick and ended up in the hospital again for an extended period. Maintaining the basic necessities of life was my responsibility, so I just went ahead and managed the money and made the decisions that kept our home intact.

THE FAMILY CONNECTION

And then there is the family connection — the added responsibility of taking care of not only your spouse, but often his family. Sometimes, it includes your family too. After all, we already had proven our capability in many ways. Certainly, that was true in my case. My growing business success meant family was calling on me to solve other problems, too. For awhile, I accepted the role of family problem solver. I hadn't yet learned my limits.

But I remember one incident in which I began to get a glimmer of those limitations. My husband and I often had small dinner parties. I enjoyed cooking. We planned such a party for several of our family members on one weekend. I flew in Friday from a consulting job on the West Coast. Friday night, I started getting ready for the party.

First, I had to clean the house. Forget the men. I knew that other women would notice that layer of dirt on the baseboards, so, already exhausted from my week's trip, I went to work with dust mop and spray cleaner in hand. I got up early to go grocery shopping for that night's menu. Then, I got a clear sign I was on overload. Preparing the food that afternoon, I suddenly realized we had no pepper, and I basically became hysterical. My husband came in, and I was sobbing.

"What's wrong?" he asked, with some concern

"We're (sob) out of (sob) pepper!" I cried.

Running back to the store to get pepper was a small chore, but at that moment it was the proverbial straw that broke the old camel's back.

"Hattie," I said to myself the next day as I lay in bed too exhausted to get up. "You need to let go of giving dinner parties. You can't do it all."

I'm not the only one who tried and failed.

 KATE. By the time Richard and I were married three years, I had added his family to my list. I was used to the responsibility of family. I was from a large family, and I accepted a caregiving role at an early age. So it seemed natural to add Richard's family to that list. His sisters listed me in their will as guardian of their children should they die prematurely. That's the level of

trust I generated. There was no doubt in anyone's mind that I would take on the responsibility and treat it seriously.

Even after Richard and I were separated, when his sister had marital problems, she chose to come stay with me, not Richard. I was the one who shored her up. Meanwhile, my own family was requiring a lot of attention. It's little wonder that I finally burned out.

 TAMARA. I come from a large family, six children in all. As the oldest girl, I helped out from an early age with my younger brothers and sisters. Being there for family was always a priority. When Phil and I were married, taking on *his* family's problems seemed normal. But those problems were enormous.

His mother, an alcoholic, moved in with us shortly after our marriage. She had no income and no place else to live. She was a difficult woman to live with. I was sympathetic to her problems, but her temper tantrums and outbursts caused a lot of stress. I finally told Phil he had to find another place for her.

Now, Phil's father lives with us. We have a separate apartment for him over the garage. He is a recluse and keeps to himself, but we go up to visit every day, each of us watching certain shows with him.

My own large family has its shares of ups and downs — marital problems, money problems, aging parents, the usual gamut in a group that large. I am still a sounding board, but I have had to learn to let loose and let each of them work their problems out without much input from me. I don't have solutions for everyone.

Sex . . . What Sex?

Most relationships start out with that magical ingredient, we called "chemistry," between the sexes. But as the parent-child relationship takes over, what started out as a playful, reciprocal sexual relationship disappears. This loss of physical intimacy between couples is difficult for both man and woman. Sometimes, it plants the seed for infidelity.

 SARAH. We probably got married because of lust. We were both in high school, and it was like, "hubba, hubba." We couldn't keep our hands off each other. The beginning of our marriage was much the same way. I got pregnant right away. He left for Vietnam. But after his return, the sex play picked right back up.

But, as I began to make more and more decisions and became the parent, all that changed. I made romantic efforts, setting up candlelight dinners on occasion, making sure birthdays and anniversaries were special and romantic. But inside, sex had diminished to an occasional biological need on my part. I tried to pretend that need signified love. We still made love occasionally, but Marvin was finding sexual playmates outside the marriage.

The first time I discovered his unfaithfulness, I threw him out. We had been married ten years at that point. And I was definitely making all the decisions by then. He moved into an apartment around the corner and courted me for six months. He called every day, sent me flowers, sent me cards, pleaded for another chance. I took him back.

But after we moved again because of my promotion, he must have started again. He went clubbing with friends I never met. In retrospect, I think many of them might have been women. But I was working so hard, I was, quite frankly, too tired to care. I just kept plugging away. On increasingly rare occasions, I would set up a romantic date. We would make love on those nights.

But the end came after almost twenty-five years of marriage. I could ignore his infidelity no longer. I found two tickets to a show in his jacket pocket. The date was for Mother's Day. Although I didn't really think so deep down, I hoped that perhaps he was planning to surprise me. On Mother's Day, I was especially sweet, taking care not to say anything that would start an argument.

At 6 o'clock, Marvin announced, "We've been together all day. I am going to go out with the guys for awhile."

"I'll come with you," I said, uncharacteristically. "I have nothing else to do now."

He tried a couple of other tacks, but when I wouldn't let him go voluntarily, he resorted to accusations.

"Why do you have to be a noose around my neck," he shouted as he left the house.

I knew by now, of course, that those tickets were for him and another woman. I drove to the theater after he left to confront him, but the tickets were sold out. I saw his car and contemplated smashing his windshield. But violence was never my style. I wrote a very nasty note. Finally, I calmed down and wrote a short note. It said, "Hope you enjoyed the show. Don't bother to come home. I changed the security code."

He was on the phone the next day, quietly pleading for forgiveness. I spent twenty-five years caring for Marvin. It's hard to shut that down. I still struggle with it, even after our divorce. But on that day, I took him back.

 TAMARA. The chemistry between Phil and I was magic. We had sex several times a day in the beginning of our relationship. It was pretty incredible. I thought of us as spiritual soul mates, not just physical ones. The combination of the two dimensions was dynamite for both of us.

But that lasted as long as Phil was pulling his weight. When he wouldn't do his share of the chores, and then wouldn't even keep up his end of the bargain in our business, I turned off. The more responsibility I took on, the less I wanted sex. Phil still wanted to make love, but I thought of it simply as an obligation. If enough time had passed, I would consent solely because I felt I had to. But I didn't really enjoy it. I don't think he did either.

AVOIDANCE—"I HAVE TO WORK LATE AGAIN"

Many of us found more and more reasons to work late. We were not happy with our relationships, but we weren't ready to face the issue. So work became a way to avoid coming face to face with our home lives. When we face the issue head on, we take a risk — the risk of the solution being different from our desire.

 SARAH. I got all my support, all my encouragement from friends at work. There I was needed, but even better, I was appreciated. My job was demanding, and I really felt I needed to be there. Once our son graduated from high school, coming home at 10 or 11 p.m. at night was not unusual for me. I didn't even realize I was avoiding the situation at home. I thought I *had* to work late.

Since my divorce, however, I find myself going home often at 6 p.m. The difference is there's no stress at home. I like being there. Now, I bring work home on weekends and work at home if I need to. I'm only beginning to realize how much of an oasis work provided for me when I wasn't willing to squarely face how much I hated my married life.

 SUE. Perhaps, that is where I am now. I find myself working late often. But John and I are fighting so much these days. Perhaps I am avoiding facing the issue. It is something I will need to think about harder. I'm not sure I really *have* to work as many hours as I do. Certainly, the company culture encourages it, but, still I have a choice, don't I?

THE WORLD IS TOO HEAVY

While the average woman can carry a child for miles, it's pretty tough to carry a 200-pound man.

The end result of carrying is exhaustion. The burden becomes too great. We can't walk another step carrying the responsibility for other adults on our shoulders. For many women carriers, this is the end of the relationship. For others, the lucky ones, it is the beginning of a changed perspective between the woman and man.

But before that end, we struggle on . . . and on . . . and on . . .

THE SIGNS OF CARRYING

There are many red flags that alert you to carrying. For example, you:

- ❏ Play the parent role
- ❏ Manage the money
- ❏ Carry other family members
- ❏ Experience changes in the sexual relationship
- ❏ Make all the decisions
- ❏ Stay busy to avoid facing the situation
- ❏ Carry most of the responsibilities
- ❏ Quit asking for help
- ❏ Feel emotionally alone
- ❏ Have a life that is unbalanced among work, family, social, self, and spiritual needs
- ❏ Feel burdened and exhausted

Are there red flags that you are carrying in your relationship?

❑

❑

❑

❑

❑

❑

❑

❑

❑

❑

❑

❑

The Four R's

Chapter 5

The Cycle Of Carrying—The Four R's

For some of us, it takes a short time to realize the relationship is not going to work if we take on all the responsibility. For others, it is a cycle — a clear pattern — that repeats itself many times before we realize that the relationship is going downhill. For too many of us, the cycle speeds up from a slow spiral into a whirling vortex before we're sucked under and exhaust our will or ability to carry.

I call this cycle the Four R's. The R's stand for *rationalize*, *reoccurrence*, *resolve*, and *resentment*. Let's look at each of them separately.

STEP 1—RATIONALIZE

The first mental step we take to become a carrier in a given situation is to rationalize why it's better for *us* to take on the particular responsibility. We have such high expectations of ourselves. We can do it better, right? My travel planning example illustrates this.

I planned all our trips and vacations. I rationalized that it made sense for me to do this, because of my extensive

---

business travel. I had all the connections. I had the free airline tickets from my frequent flyer mileage. I knew the travel agents. I had the hotel connections. All of this was true. But in the process, we were no longer operating as a team, making joint decisions on vacations. I was planning the entire trip.

STEP 2—REOCCURRENCE

Soon, we find that whatever rationalization started us on this road, the process keeps happening again and again, even long after the initial reasoning doesn't fit.

In my case, I found myself planning trips I didn't even need to be involved in. When my husband and I were first married, we returned to his hometown every year for his annual family reunion. In the beginning of our marriage, my husband made all the arrangements. Generally, we stayed with his parents. Often, we drove. But even if we were on a tight schedule and needed to fly, he called and booked the flight. For my husband, this was the equivalent of Christmas. He never missed it.

As time went on, I found myself taking over the process. I was booking the flight. As we became more affluent, I was booking a hotel also, rather than staying with my husband's parents. It certainly wasn't an event I needed to take over. This was my husband's annual event.

STEP 3—RESOLVE

Some women never get to step three. As it becomes apparent that the event is going to reoccur frequently, they stop. But for many of us, resolve sets the stage for the reoccurring pattern. We simply resolve ourselves to taking on this responsibility permanently. Our rationalization process lead us to thinking this is the easiest route all the way around to handle the situation. Short-term, that is probably true. Long-term, we all lose.

By the time I was married five years, I had resolved that I would always make the trip arrangements, regardless of where we were going. I had taken over. And my husband was glad to have me take over. It was one less item on his list of responsibilities.

STEP 4—RESENTMENT

Resentment is sneaky. Having resolved to do this job, we often find a quiet resentment creeping in that we didn't count upon. For me, I began to resent doing everything. For the man, as he relinquishes responsibility, he resents having his individual rights usurped. In effect, he has given up power and autonomy. That causes resentment that he, too, probably didn't expect.

My building resentment about the imbalance of responsibilities in our marriage boiled over one fateful year before the annual family reunion. I was tired of making all the travel arrangements. I resented always having to think about where we were going next and what we were going to do when we got there. That year, I simply didn't plan the trip. I didn't tell my husband. I just didn't lift a finger. By the time my husband realized it, it was too late to make hotel and flight arrangements. To say he was angry would be an understatement. In my husband's mind, missing the family reunion was not an option. The fight that ensued was not pretty.

We called the family to say hello but never discussed the reunion. His silence on the subject was indicative of his anger. Afterwards, I returned to the old cycle. I rationalized that, indeed, we should have been there, and resolved to make the arrangements well in advance for the next year. I just swallowed the resentment. And so, the process repeated itself again in an endless loop that seemingly has no end.

Many of the other women were caught in the same loop.

MARIA AND JOE—TWO INCOMES OR ONE?

I constantly rationalize my husband's lack of business acumen. He is a fine plumber and a nice person. But he doesn't handle the business money end well. We run a money cycle that constantly goes through all the 4 R's. Because of Joe's lack of money sense, I have kept my checking account separate from his from the beginning. He comes to me when money is tight. When I ask why, it's always because something happened he didn't plan on. So, I take money out of my account to float him through again. It's a constant go-around with us.

Since our baby was born, though, the resentment is growing on my part. Part of me wants to quit my job and be a full-time mother. We worked hard for this precious baby. I went through hell with doctors and fertility medication to bring this child into the world. I would like to stay home and cuddle and nurture our son.

Of course, that's not a possibility on Joe's current income. I know that.

But, then, I think, perhaps I could stay home if Joe would go to work for someone else who manages *their* business well. Joe is a fine plumber and would do an outstanding job. We would have health benefits and not be dependent on mine. We would have a steady, reliable source of income and could plan a budget.

So, the resentment is there. But then, the resolve flips in. Oh well, I think, I've worked for fifteen years and I've enjoyed it. Maybe I would hate being at home. So, OK, this is best and I will keep working without complaint.

And then, something goes wrong again, and he needs money. Boom, I'm back to resenting his lack of business acumen. We are in a loop, no doubt about it.

JOAN AND ALLEN—GOOD INTENTIONS ARE NOT ENOUGH

I rationalized from day one that I didn't need financial support. I had been on my own supporting myself and my two children for seven years. I knew Allen was pretty naive about the amount of money it took to support us. At first, that was all right with me. I saw his wonderful qualities. He was loving and supportive of my ambitions and willing to support me emotionally. He was loyal to the idea of family and had a wonderful sense of humor. Being with him was always fun.

I also rationalized that when we had a child, his ambitions would rev up. He was well educated with a masters degree. We agreed to have one child, although I wasn't anxious to start a new family. My own children were just reaching the age, ten and twelve years old, where they didn't require constant care. I was looking forward to the end of the search for good baby-sitters. But Allen wanted a child. I thought that if he was willing to be a stepfather to my children, the least I could do was give him a child that would call him "daddy" instead of "Allen." So, we agreed to have another child.

But when our son was born, the employment situation was no better for Allen. He kept hitting dead-end jobs. We remained dependent on my income. The cycle continued. So, I resolved that I was indeed the family breadwinner. It was up to me. I started my own business to build the company I originally thought my husband might build.

The resentment came out in my control. Since I was the chief financial support, I felt free to make all the financial decisions and to delegate duties at home. But, we weren't a team. Allen's resentment came out in subtle ways. If I asked him to do a chore, like fix the garage door, he would say yes and then just not do it. Weeks would pass. Nothing would happen. He became the master stonewaller.

This was the cycle. We were definitely in a slow, downward spiral, not really facing the issues.

SUE AND JOHN—MR. MOM

I know we rationalized from the beginning of our marriage, also. I was a business major in college. John was an artist — creative, free-spirited. We indeed personified that old folk tale that opposites attract. John was the primary breadwinner at first. But when the local economy took a nose dive and his business went south, we rationalized that we would switch roles for awhile. John would take care of the kids, and I would temporarily bring home the family paycheck.

It was great for awhile. John's artistry came out in a redecorated home, gourmet cooking, a landscaped yard. And there was no way I could take on the travel my career required without John taking on the responsibilities of chauffeuring the kids to activities, doctor appointments, and grocery shopping. So, the cycle reoccurred and reoccurred. With each cycle, John became more the at-home parent. I became more the financial support.

But it wasn't planned. What was supposed to be temporary became permanent. John feels today he has too much responsibility for transporting the kids to get a full-time job. Yet he also resents not being the primary wage earner. For him, it is an embarrassment. Ten years ago, he was making good money as an interior designer. Today, he resents the position he is in.

I am resentful also. I never really intended to bring home the principal paycheck. I feel like he's not living up to his potential and our marriage contract. I have missed too much of my children's activities. I am not there to be of comfort to them when they need a hand to hold onto. I feel trapped. I have the career. John is down to part-time work as a subcontractor for another company. I want him to work for someone full-time. But he doesn't want to take a boring job, like designing interiors for a cookie-cutter home builder in a new subdivision.

We go around and around.

Now, we've reached the point where we are saying things to each other we didn't say earlier. Hurtful stuff. I do it to him. And he does it to me. I've thrown it up to his face that I am the financial support in an argument. I know that's a hot button for him and yet, I push it. He yells at me for not calling home and saying I will be late in time to postpone dinner or cook for fewer people. It's a classic role reversal.

Both of us still want this marriage to work in spite of all the challenges. We are approaching our 25th anniversary. Our kids want a complete family that nurtures them all the way into adulthood. We need to break this cycle, but neither of us is sure how to go about it.

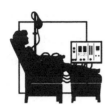

MADDIE AND LIONEL—FACING PEER PRESSURE

Financially, I carried the load from the beginning. It was my house. I bought it before we were married. I paid the bills. What I wanted was a companion. As a dialysis patient, I thought I would never have a lover or a companion. To have found one in Lionel was enough.

Lionel wanted me to carry the load financially. That was fine with him. But that meant I also carried a lot of power. And that wasn't fine with his friends. His friends on the street would say, "How come you let your old lady keep all the cash?" "How come you let your woman do this . . . or do that?" So, I guess in some way he was influenced by that. The resentment started building in him.

I was in the hospital a lot. Dialysis weakens a person in other ways. At times, I was in the hospital for various problems, including a hysterectomy, glaucoma surgery, and surgery for a kidney transplant which later failed. That failure was a terrible blow for me. My friends would come to visit me, and say "Where's Lionel? How come we are here to visit you and he isn't? Kick his butt out, Maddie."

When he wasn't there for my illnesses, the resentment built even more. I thought somehow he might take more responsibility when I was sick. But he didn't. If he did show up, it was generally to bring me the bills, so that I could pay them from my hospital bed.

But I was resolved with a capital R. Lionel was my friend before he was my lover and husband. "He's a good man," I told my friends. I never talked to Lionel about it. And so the cycle continued.

SARAH AND MARVIN—THE FIXER

I am a fixer. Every time Marvin complained, I tried to fix the situation. I even let him quit his jobs just in the hopes that he would quit complaining with a new one. I always rationalized that next time he would be happy. Well, he never was. Always something was wrong — his boss was a jerk, the company policies were stupid, it didn't pay enough, the hours were too long — there was always a reason the job was terrible. The last fifteen years of our marriage was just a reoccurring cycle of that scenario.

Every time I resolved to find the answer. I encouraged Marvin to change careers when he complained about the hours and low pay of being a mechanic. I encouraged him to start his own business when he brought it up. I encouraged and encouraged. Maybe I even pushed on occasion.

Resentment built on both sides, but particularly on Marvin's side. He resented my success as senior vice president at a computer company and my control. Early on, he began to blame me. For example, Marvin blamed me for sidetracking his career when I moved the family to a new city to take advantage of a promotion. "You always have to have your way," he said often.

And once again I resolved to help him find an answer. By the time we were married ten years, the pattern was petrified into place.

TAMARA AND PHIL—THE TROOPER

I really wanted the marriage between Phil and I to work. After all, this was a second marriage for me. So, when he turned out to be less responsible than I imagined him to be, I began rationalizing. I just set my jaw and got to work. As a single mom, I had done all the chores *and* worked. So, OK, if Phil wasn't willing to pitch in, I could just continue doing that. So, while Phil did nothing, I cooked. And cleaned and fed the pets. And shopped. The kids are bigger now, I reasoned. *They* can pitch in more.

But it wasn't easy to be cleaning the bathroom while Phil played tennis with his buddies. Or to be grocery shopping late at night while he watched television. Underneath, I was really resentful. But I didn't say anything. He already had made it clear that he wasn't interested in pitching in.

His response was generally, "It's all right if the bathroom is dirty. Just don't do it." Well, that didn't suit me. I can only stand so much dirt, and the house was already dirtier than I liked. I just didn't have time to keep up with it.

The more I did, however, the less inclination Phil had to pitch in. Then, when the same cycle began to occur in our business, the resentment really grew. I worked long hours designing ads and brochures for clients. Phil was working fewer and fewer hours, choosing instead to play racquetball and tennis during office hours.

But I was also resolved to make this marriage work. So I just did more and more. It couldn't last forever, though, and it didn't. Eventually, Phil's irresponsibility was too much. I couldn't cycle through one more round.

The scene was set for a show down.

Chapter 6

When The Cycle Stops—
Turning Points

Carrying often ends when we are exhausted, worn out. We are burned out, broken down to where we can carry no more. But the negative impact of carrying starts before then. We have already mentioned the change in our sex lives — from lovers and playmates, to dutiful fulfillers of sexual drive at best, and unfaithfulness at worst. We have talked about the control of one person over another.

It boils down to lack of trust. The carrier no longer trusts her partner to fulfill her expectations — any expectations.

The vacation? If we don't plan it, it doesn't happen. So, we get out the calendars, block out the dates, call the travel agent, or take the car in to be serviced. We research the best prices, what to do at our destination, figure out the budget. We inventory what we need, make the shopping trip for clothes or sundries, pack the bags. Then, by the time the vacation starts, we are exhausted.

Child care? We do it. We keep the family schedule, inform our husbands when and where to transport them if we can't get away from work to do it ourselves. Because we don't trust our husbands to remember the schedule, we call thirty minutes before they are to pick up the child, and remind them.

Finances? At some point, we discovered our spouses would overspend and lose control of the checkbook, and we would get Not Sufficient Funds notices from our banks. We don't trust them to keep up on the quarterly income taxes, because, quite frankly, they let it go in the past before we took over. So we pay the bills, reconcile the checking account, worry about the budget, put our husbands on an allowance, and cut back on credit cards.

Home maintenance? We handle those projects, too. At midnight we are doing laundry. On Saturdays, we are mowing the lawn and cleaning. We call the plumber and the appliance repair service. We track the periodic maintenance due on our air conditioning and heating units and call for service.

Extended family? We keep up with them also. We plan when to visit the in-laws, our parents, and schedule the trips. We remind our husbands to call his parents. When the in-laws visit, we plan the meals, cook the food, and schedule the recreational outings.

Work? Yes, we do that too. Our husbands can't be counted on to provide financially, either. They have changed jobs too often, and let us down when we most needed the support. We can't rely on them to provide continuous support. So, we pursue our careers with a fervor, work late, and take courses to advance us up the ranks.

Little wonder we burn out. Superwoman is a myth, not a model. Every time we take on one new commitment and complete it, we pat ourselves on the back and take on one more. But the resentment is growing. For most women, there is a turning point when they know they can go no further. Something has to change.

HATTIE—THE $300 PHONE CALL

I was in South Africa, teaching a roomful of Afrikaner corporate executives how to relate to people of color. It was a tough assignment. And I was alone in a strange country with no friends close at hand. It gave me plenty of time to think. I was thinking about my growing business, the increasing gap between my husband and me caused by that business, his increasing reliance on me to take charge of everything.

And not just my husband relied on me. I was, by this point, the most successful alumni of our tiny rural Arkansas high school and a bit of a celebrity in our farming community. My family was now calling on me when they needed help. So were old friends and neighbors.

One night, I woke up at 3 a.m. at my wits' end and called my husband. And I just started to cry. I don't cry often, but this was a real torrent — the kind of crying where you are sobbing from deep in your gut, and the words come out in gasps between sobs. "Everybody calls me," I sobbed, "my family, my friends. But who am I supposed to call? I'm supposed to call you, but you aren't there anymore."

My accountant husband was quiet through all my sobbing, interjecting an occasional, "Hmmmm," in response. At the time, I blamed him for not responding with emotion. I mean, I was falling apart.

In retrospect, though, I realize I had as much to do with our situation as he did. I built this package myself from scratch, and I didn't like it, and it hurt from the inside out. The marriage didn't end at that point. We shared religious values that made commitment to marriage a strong bond. But after another two years, we knew we had to separate for both of us to grow. In reality, though, I made that decision in a $300 long distance sob fest from a South African hotel room. That was my turning point.

 ### SARAH—THE LAST STRAW – JAIL

The final straw came for me shortly before our twenty-fifth wedding anniversary. Our daughter was grown, my husband was unemployed, but I was increasingly independent. I was going on a trip with a girlfriend. We planned it for months, and I was pumped about this trip. One week before I was to leave, I got a phone call. Actually, I had seven phone calls — messages stacked up on our answering machine as I arrived home. Marvin was calling from jail. Someone had cut him off while he was driving, and, at the stop light, Marvin had jumped out of his car, rushed up to the car that had cut him off, opened the door, grabbed the driver, and hit him full force with his fist.

As I put down the phone, I covered my head with my hands and tried to comprehend. Who was this man? Marvin had been a whiner, a complainer, a quitter. But he was not violent. I was numb. I knew we had crossed over a line. I could go no further.

Several phone calls later, I found an attorney at home who could post the $1,000 bond the next morning. By that time, I was thinking that the man my husband assaulted might well sue us. Should I cancel my trip, I wondered? As I sat in the waiting room at the jail waiting for Marvin to appear, and trying to comprehend what to me was a surreal experience, I knew I would go on my trip. Nothing Marvin did would impact my life further.

My rescuing days were over.

As we drove home, I told him that I was filing for divorce. I also said I would stay three more months to give him time to find a job. But then I was gone. I don't think he believed me, but I was serious. I left in three months, taking only my car, my clothes and my computer. He had the house and everything in it we had purchased over twenty-five years. I didn't want to argue over any of it. I just wanted out.

MADDIE—INFIDELITY BREAKS THE BOND

I could handle anything but unfaithfulness. I went into the relationship knowing that Lionel was a part-time worker. He held construction jobs when he needed to, but his heart was in his music. He played in a band that was doing well on the local scene. As the lead singer, he naturally attracted women but I trusted him on this issue. For one thing, he always introduced me to the crowd, pointing me out as his wife.

But I couldn't make every gig the band played. Between my dialysis treatments and my job commitments, I missed quite a few.

About five years ago, I noticed Lionel was not as affectionate. He would come home in the evenings and go straight into the bedroom to change and wash his face. No hugs and kisses at the door. I had an ugly premonition.

One afternoon, I dropped by my mother-in-law's home. She was sitting outside at a picnic table conversing with a woman. When they saw me, the woman got up quickly, grabbed two small children, and left before I could come over and say hello. I had seen this woman before at Lionel's gigs. When I asked my mother-in-law who she was, my mother-in-law simply said she was a neighbor. But I could tell she was lying from the way she said it.

Not long after, I asked Lionel if he was having an affair. He got up angrily without answering and left the room. Later, I found out he had gone into the living room. He was sitting in the dark crying because he didn't know how to answer me.

He *was* having an affair. He was seeing the woman with two kids, a welfare mom with no job and little prospect of one. Not long after, he came home and told me what I really didn't want to hear. "I'm not happy," he said. "I'm leaving."

I found myself sitting on the floor, crying hard, and asking, "What did I do?" "What did I do to deserve this?"

That was the turning point in the cycle. When he left, I picked myself up, and thought to myself: "Maddie, you came to peace about being alone a long time ago. Long before Lionel came into your life. You have a job. You have your church. You have your faith. You can return to that life. It's a good life." Within just twenty-four hours, I was set to go forward without him.

JOAN—HITTING THE WALL

The realization that I would not duplicate the financial success of my successful, businessman father was devastating. For seven years, I poured my heart and soul into forming a business that would grow into an entity larger than me — I immersed myself in business plans, talked with venture capitalists, set up alliances with major corporations. Facing downsizing after my major expansion partner, a bank, was taken over by the Federal Insurance Deposit Corporation, I was tired, very, very tired.

For years, I felt I had to be the primary breadwinner. For years, I felt the weight of that responsibility.

After selling the business for a fraction of its potential worth only a year before, I went home. I was exhausted, mentally and physically. I had hit the wall. I also wanted to be home with our son. My two older children were in college, and I didn't want to sacrifice my last child to the loneliness of a latch-key existence. I decided to take a sabbatical from the business world and write a book I had wanted to write for several years.

That decision placed my husband and me in new roles. When we sold the company, he was also out of work. After a series of jobs, he had joined our company. Nothing in his employment history gave me confidence and trust that he would be able to take up the slack and provide a standard of living that matched our current needs. But, I didn't have a choice. I couldn't carry the load any further. That was my turning point.

TAMARA—THE BANKRUPTCY BLUES

Bankruptcy was the end of the downward spiral for Phil and me. I was willing to do almost anything to make this second marriage work. I carried the business for both of us, meeting deadlines and producing advertisements, brochures, and other marketing material for our clients. I carried the household, shopping, cooking, cleaning, helping the children as best I could with their homework and activities.

But watching Phil desert his responsibilities day by day was too much for me. He slept late, missed deadlines, and missed meetings. From my vantage point, he didn't seem to care at all about what happened to us. He had taken over the finances when we got married, and too late, I realized how deeply in debt we had fallen.

The turning point came when I realized we would lose our home. I had wanted a home for a long time. Now, because of Phil's financial mismanagement, we were behind on payments. And there was no money to make those payments.

It took what little courage I had left to ask Phil to leave. I still loved him. And after facing the humiliation of bankruptcy in the community, I also had to face the devastation of a failed second marriage. But I could not go on with the marriage as it stood at that low point. I no longer trusted Phil. To survive, I needed to pour all my energies into work and the children. I couldn't carry him, too. Not any longer.

KATE—ISSUING NEW RULES

In retrospect, the end of our marriage came when Richard came home to tell me one evening that he wanted to move out for six months and think about his life, our marriage, and his future. It was a murky ending, however. First, Richard didn't move. For the next six months, we lived in limbo in the same house, running parallel but unconnected lives. Finally, I took charge, as usual. Living under the same roof in a pretend state of *life as usual* was just too stressful. I told him if he wanted six months separation to think about his life and future, then the clock was now ticking. Move.

It took him a month to find an apartment but he moved. I would see him when he came to visit our five-year-old daughter, but he said nothing further about his plans. Once again, I took the initiative and asked him what he thought about us as a couple. He was non-definitive.

In the meantime, I began to do well financially with my tutoring business, and I was doing well in graduate school, also. I became very active in a singles group at my church. I was making new friends.

A few more months passed, and Richard appeared at my door. "I think I want to come home," he said.

"Oh? What's different now?" I asked.

Richard explained that he thought he was really missing something in life by being married, but he now had changed his mind. Being on his own turned out to be tough. He was ready to move back in that night.

My life, however, was much less stressful. I developed new interests and friends now that I wasn't carrying Richard. I wasn't so ready to accept the old rules. But I was willing to try, given new circumstances. I explained to Richard that if he moved back home, the old rules wouldn't apply anymore. I explained some of my needs. I told him that we would have to start marriage counseling immediately.

"I need to think about that," he said. Then, he disappeared on me.

I finally called.

"I took what you said and put it into the formula, and it just didn't work," he finally told me. "I don't think I can live with those new rules."

"Fine," I said. "Do you want to file the divorce papers or should I?"

It's no surprise that I was the one to finally file for divorce although Richard initiated the subject a year and a half earlier by announcing his decision to leave.

MARIA—THE BABY

For us, the turning point has been our newborn baby. We worked hard to have this child. He is a great blessing, and we both want him to have a good life. But it was more a turning point for Joe than for me. He told me, "I never had to think about anyone except myself. If I needed a dime, I would get work and earn that dime. I never had to take responsibility for someone's future. I want to learn how to do that."

The net result is we have begun to make real progress in our relationship. I can see progress in Joe's attitude. He wants to be a father, a family man.

Many women have not yet reached a turning point, a moment when they knew that the relationship must change or end. This was true for Sue who was facing the subtle evolution of a marriage into roles with which neither was comfortable. John and Sue both wanted the relationship to go forward. But how?

Much soul-searching by all of these women led to some solutions and some triumphs.

TURNING POINTS

These women experienced a variety of turning points that prompted them to action.

❑ Infidelity
❑ No communication
❑ Lack of emotional support
❑ Expectations not fulfilled
❑ Financial disaster
❑ Partner unwilling to renegotiate
❑ Added responsibilities
❑ Trust weakened or gone

Have you reached a turning point in your relationship?

❑
❑
❑

Chapter 7

The Solutions

Not all of the women ended up in divorce court. For some of us, like me, Sarah, and Kate, it was too late. We saw no other way out. Others were still in the throes of unresolved issues. They wanted their relationships to work. Those of us who were divorced wanted to make sure we didn't repeat past mistakes.

Fortunately, we were past blaming just our men. We knew that to go forward we first had to take a look at ourselves and take responsibility for the part *we* played in the relationship's demise and make some changes.

There were similar types of changes among us all.

Let Loose. One change was the willingness to let loose of some of their responsibilities, truly share decisions, and in the process, give up some control. To do so, the women had to allow for some failure. They also had to compromise on their insistence of a rigid time frame. The attitude of do it now, or I'll do it, did not work. They also had to recognize where they could compromise and accept the differences.

Communicate. Another was learning to better communicate. This starts with listening. As one of my friends said, "A good listener is not only popular with everyone, but after awhile she gets to know something." Busy women are not always good listeners. They need to learn to communicate their feelings and expectations in a positive way. They need to recognize their needs and the needs of their spouse. Good communication involves risk, and, at least in the beginning, it is often painful. The risk comes from not knowing the outcome. Sometimes, when we bring issues to the surface to be explored, we don't like the reality we find. For some, communication may mean separating. For others, communication brings a renewed cohesiveness. We are forced to deal with issues we have been ignoring. And with good communication comes a constant renegotiation of the contract. Life is not static. Neither is marriage.

Love. Another was the solvent of love. Love is a verb. We choose to love, and tender communication is the key to good communication. Giving heart-felt compliments when there were changes for the better, stroking, laughter — all lead to reconciliation. Many of the women had to relearn how to play, bringing with it a sweet renewal of love and physical intimacy.

Spiritual Strength. Finally, there was an underlying current of spiritual strength that provided us the faith to go forward. Knowing ourselves, being in touch with our inner soul makes all the difference. A trust in God led to a trust in events. A trust in God enabled the women to let loose. Each woman achieved this in her own way — some through meditation, some through prayer, some through their church affiliations or personal search.

THOSE WHO CHOSE TO STAY TOGETHER

Many of the women had changed, and the relationship had changed in the process. They felt that their marriages were now strong and on a positive forward path. Of course, it takes two. In these women's cases, the men were equally willing to take a hard look at their behavior and make changes also. And each of the resolutions reflected the individuality and uniqueness of those couples and their needs.

TAMARA—FIRST STEP, COMMUNICATE

Communicate. The first step in putting together a healthy relationship for Phil and me was communication. After we separated, we really did not communicate at all for eight months. He would call, but I had so much anger and hurt that he threw everything away, I couldn't talk to him.

At Christmas, he went to New York to see his dad.

Everything was done for the holidays. I was really kind of depressed. Christmas felt empty. Susie, my little daughter, came in to my bedroom, and asked if her stepdad, Phil, was coming home for Christmas. "I really wish he could be here." Something in her voice penetrated the wall I had built. Suddenly, the good memories, all the good times, came flooding into my consciousness.

"Tell you what," I replied. "I'll call him and see if he wants to come."

He did. He flew in on Christmas Eve, and Christmas Day was a wonderful, wonderful day filled with love and laughter. After lunch, Phil turned to me and said, "I know I've blown it. I want you to know that for the first time I am willing to do whatever it takes to patch things up." It was a Christmas miracle.

I had never heard him say that before. He was never willing to go to therapy or talk with a marriage counselor before. His pride was too great.

If he's willing to go to a marriage counselor, then there is hope, I thought. So I was willing to try again. Phil kept his bargain. He was as open and honest as he could be. The therapist was able to identify a major communication gap between us.

Phil came from a home managed (badly) by an alcoholic mother and an absent father. When his salesman father returned on Friday nights to find his wife boozed, arguments would ensue and, often, his father beat his mother. Arguments in the family were loud, often abusive. They worked things out through screaming.

In my family, nobody raised their voice. You never talked about your emotions. If you were angry, that was your problem. You just dealt with it yourself. My mom and dad never fought in front of us kids.

Neither Phil nor I realized what an impact this had on our communication system. When something was really bothering me, I would quietly say to him, "It really upset me when. . . What Phil would hear was . . . nothing. No screaming. No message. So, the anger built inside me. And built inside me.

On the other hand, when Phil would get angry he would yell. He was never physically abusive. But the yelling scared me, and I would retreat. I just went out of my way not to anger him. So communication stopped.

We learned to communicate. Phil learned that when I said something, it was important to listen — really listen. I, in turn, quit holding back. I learned to be more up front and outspoken about my thoughts and feelings. So, now we can really learn and listen from each other. And we are reaching solutions to problems as they occur, instead of letting them fester and grow in darkness.

Let Loose. The second step for me was letting loose of responsibilities. When we first married, Phil would not do anything around the house. My son cut the grass. I pretty much did the rest — cooking, shopping, laundry, dishes. I was so busy making a living that I just learned to look past a dirty house. But I was very angry about it inside.

After we started really talking, and Phil was really listening, we made a list of everything that needed to be done every week and split the list down the middle. Phil never believed all those chores were really necessary, but he was willing to do them based on my strong feelings about the need to clean up our home. I let him pick out what he wanted. I took the rest.

Now, Phil's hands-on experience has revolutionized his attitude and his behavior. He understands how much energy it takes to keep a house going, and he has assumed ever more responsibility for doing chores.

Financially, we are still struggling. Phil finished his masters degree in creative writing and became a teacher. It takes both our incomes to barely make ends meet. But we are tackling this issue together now. We met with a financial planner. We now have a plan to first, pay off school debts from the children's college expenses, then, to pay off our mortgage, and third, to set aside funds for retirement. Keeping to this plan requires a budgetary discipline that Phil has never exercised before. We don't eat out. We rent videos rather than going to first-run movies. We shop for bargains. If the dishwasher breaks and repairs are not in the budget, we wash dishes by hand until we can pay cash. We don't use credit.

I learned the value of independent opinion. But bringing in a third party (the financial planner) and devising a plan together has given Phil ownership. I am not enforcing it on him. And we are making financial progress. Our debts will soon be paid off.

Spiritual Strength. The centering prayer and meditation I practice in the morning has always been my inner strength. If I miss that quiet time, I feel it.

When we were first married, Phil and I looked for a mutual church home where we would both be comfortable. But after awhile, he quit going, and I returned to the Catholic Church where I grew up. After we reconciled, Phil agreed to convert to Catholicism. But it wasn't perfect. Phil's faith was very intellectual, in which he would read and think intellectually about God, but if he couldn't reason his way to understanding, it didn't work for him. After awhile, he once again quit going to church.

I didn't push. I have learned not to push. Part of this growing process is learning where to compromise and accepting the differences between us. But I was praying. I prayed everyday that Phil could take his faith to a deeper level — into his soul where it is more holistic.

It's happening. We began to meet with a small group from our church in our home on Sunday evenings. Sharing our day-to-day and faith experiences on a regular basis has been enlightening. I don't think men have many occasions to share deeply with one another the way women often do. I am seeing major changes in Phil's attitude. He's more helpful and unselfish. He likes church again and feels part of that community. He's more loving.

Love. Love was the foundation of our marriage from the start. But we forgot how to play during our troubled period. We are still on a tight budget, so we can't play in the sense of going on honeymoon-type vacations. But our sex life is the best it has ever been. In the past, sex just didn't work for me. Mostly, I thought . . . "well, it's been awhile since we had sex, so I guess I should do this," when Phil approached me. Now, we make love. I feel loved. I feel so incredibly loved. I want sex. I've never had that feeling before . . . ever. The better we are in other areas of our life, the better our sex life is.

With harmony in the home, laughing is easy. Joy is always right there. Sex just follows naturally.

JOAN—FIRST, LET LOOSE

Let Loose: For me, it started with letting loose. I had to let loose of the idea that *I* had to be the one to support the family. I entered our marriage thinking I was the primary breadwinner. I thought that might change after our son was born. But Allen, in spite of his best efforts, just seemed to hit a dead-end. A public relations firm he joined went out of business. A second firm went under. And then a third company went bankrupt.

But when *my* business plans went awry, I just couldn't keep going at the same pace. I had hit that wall, and I had to take some time off. Not that I trusted Allen to do the job. Nothing from his past said he would be able to step up to the plate and hit a home run. Or even get on base for that matter. I just knew I couldn't.

Spiritual Strength. Even though I didn't trust Allen to provide a living, I did trust God. Over the past fifteen years, I had been on a spiritual search to better understand God. I was learning to pray in a manner that was effective. I was more at peace than at an earlier time in my life, when I took on the entire responsibility and suffered from the stress that caused. And I have seen God's law in action. Every time we had a financial need and I prayed to see that need supplied, it was. I learned to listen for the angel thoughts, God's ideas, that led to taking the action needed to meet our needs.

So, even though I can't honestly say I directly trusted Allen to provide for us financially, I did trust God to provide and believed that God would give Allen answers just as He had me. As for my role, as I prayed I became more convinced that I needed to be more of a mother to our young son, be more available for community and church work. I saw clearly the need for more balance in my life. To do that, I had to work less.

At first, my husband panicked. He was willing, but he didn't have any source of income at that moment, either. He tried a new business unrelated to his former occupation that only threw us into deeper debt. But he was praying, too. He decided to go back to his original training. He started a financial communications firm, working out of the house. After a few months, he formed an alliance with a major national competitor. The start was slow, but business has been steadily growing.

Meanwhile, what started out as one book for me has turned into a book publishing business, helping others get their books printed and to market.

Between us, our income is returning to its former level. But my income is secondary to his now. Letting loose has taken off the pressure.

Communicate. This aspect continues to be a challenge for me. Learning to act rather than react and to communicate my feelings is an ongoing challenge. A recent example will explain.

My husband came into my home office to tell me his brother and sister would be coming up for a four-day visit. My reaction was explosive. "How could you invite them here now?" I demanded. It wasn't that I didn't want to see them. But I was involved in a major project on a short deadline. When he announced their coming, I mentally took on the responsibility for the visit. In my mind, I would now have to plan meals, go shopping for groceries, entertain my nieces, and cook for the whole gang.

There was a good reason for the visit. My husband's parents need full-time care now and they were coming to visit possible assisted living residences where my in-laws might live. I knew that. Still, I thought the timing was all wrong.

After thinking it over, though, I realized that once again I had assumed control. I had just automatically assumed responsibility for everyone's well-being. I didn't need to do that. I apologized for my outburst. Then I explained my dilemma. Together we forged a solution. We decided that the visit could be done in two days, not four. My husband called and explained to his brother and sister my work schedule and that I would only be available for dinner one evening, and that I would be working other times.

Letting loose is an on-going challenge. But I am making progress. And our relationship is becoming a partnership.

Love. Loving my husband is easy. He is inherently and naturally a kind man. But I am learning to be kinder, also. I notice when he does something nice, and I thank him.

Just that small effort on my part has made our life more loving, more harmonious.

We're still working on finding time to play together. We have canceled our vacation more than once due to work deadlines. But we look for opportunities to have dates — go to the movies or go to dinner. As we learn to enjoy one another again as companions, our sex life is getting better — more spontaneous, more relaxed.

MADDIE—FIRST, A RENEWAL OF ROMANCE

Maddie's situation is different, because her expectations are different. She went into the marriage expecting to carry the financial load, and that expectation has not changed. She wanted a companion, someone she could count on to be there.

Love. This is the area that is most improved for us. Lionel really courts me. He is very romantic. I will come home at night, and there will be music playing, pillows on the floor beside a bottle of wine, candles burning. I feel like a young, beautiful woman. What makes it especially wonderful is that I missed that in my younger days due to illness. Often, Lionel will call me at work and invite me to dinner. And dinner will be at a lovely restaurant with soft lighting.

Even more important, he is there. He is always there. When I hurt from dialysis treatments, he holds me and cuddles me. Words cannot express how important it is for me to have someone there to soothe the pain. It is all I ever wanted. I am content.

Spiritual Strength. From high school on, when my illness first surfaced, I have turned to God for strength. Regardless of the difficulty, it is my faith that God is there to hold, guide, and guard me that gives me the strength to go on. When Lionel was unfaithful, my faith gave me the strength to deal with it, the strength to tell him to leave, and the strength to accept him back when he told me he valued our marriage and wanted to stay. But I don't lean on Lionel, anymore. I keep focused on God.

Communicate. Lionel has yet to tell me he had an affair. But, in some ways, he has shown me he has changed. He has given up the band. Now, he works a 40-hour week at a company. He's here at night to talk to me. He often takes me to my dialysis treatments. We laugh a lot. We are more honest about our expectations with one another. Still, I keep a close watch. Not all doubt has been erased. Perhaps it is because he has never admitted to the affair.

MARIA—FIRST, COMMUNICATE

Communicate. When he got overwhelmed or depressed, Joe would shut down emotionally and just not talk to me. My reaction was to be resentful because I felt like I was the one carrying the load for all of us. I'd be thinking that if it weren't for me, we wouldn't have a house. If it weren't for me, we wouldn't have a car. If it weren't for me, we wouldn't have a thing. Why am I the only one that is responsible? Why am I the only one that cares?

The baby has changed Joe's attitude, though. He is really trying to communicate. And I spend time explaining my feelings and needs to him. He has begun to spend time explaining his feelings to me.

In the past, he would sometimes lie to me. He might tell me he had the money for something when he did not. He might tell me he was working when he was actually at the bar with his friends. I told him that his lying was hurting us more than his lack of responsibility. I guess since I play the role of parent so often, he was playing the role of child, similar to a 10-year-old telling his mom he had done his homework when he had not as he goes out the door to play with his friends.

We are getting past that. Joe now tells me when he does something he knows I won't like, such as stopping to have drinks with his friends on his way home. And I have to remember that I told him I would rather hear the truth and not react with anger. Instead, I thank him for telling me, and then wait for a time to discuss the fact that I need him home more to help out with child care.

He understands now that it's important not to blindside me on money. I never see money from Joe. But I hand him bills and say you need to pay this. Like the car payment. He makes the car payment, now. And if he doesn't have the money for an item, he'll tell me, rather than just letting it go. I still loan him money, but he's paying me back when he can.

And I still want him to make the house payment. He knows that, but he says he can't do it yet. I wonder what makes him think I can? Because I've done it from the get-go? But I knew when I married him what he was like about money. So, if I get angry, I need to be angry with myself. That cools my frustration. I just remember his wonderful qualities that first attracted me and I'm grateful for the progress we've made.

Let Loose. I've also had to let loose of my time frame on lots of projects. I'm like the mechanic's wife with the car that doesn't run. He has all these skills, but we've had a leaky kitchen faucet for months. On the other hand, I quit asking him to clean out the garage, and one day he just went out and did it. I'm discovering that if I express my wishes and then let loose of my desire to have it done right then, Joe will get around to it eventually.

I'm also trying to let him work out his own business challenges. He recently got the plumbing contract on a huge renovation project, but he didn't have the money he needed to buy supplies. He went to the bank, but they turned him down, saying the contract wasn't enough collateral to qualify for a loan. I just stayed out of it. He started the job, and I asked him how he got the money.

Joe told me he went to the vendors and asked them to wait for payment until he got paid. They were willing to do that. That's real progress. It made me realize he is accepting responsibility.

Love. Putting the love in communications is the honey that is soothing us over the rough spots. The more reasons I found to compliment him, the more he stepped up to the plate. It's not a case of parenting. It's a case of love. I tell him he is good at what he does. And then ask, how do we channel that skill into something positive? And then, I step back and let him figure it out without interference. I am a strong person, and I have a tendency to say, let me do it because then I know it will be right.

I am doing the same now with home chores. I just plant a seed and tell him how much it means to me to have a nice yard, or whatever. When he does it, I am appreciative. And I really am. He does more and more, because the appreciation is there. Love is the honey that sweetens our life.

❏ ❏ ❏

THOSE WHO GO IT ALONE

For the women who divorced, changes by both parties was not a viable option. Change for the individual, however, was very much an option.

❏ ❏ ❏

HATTIE—FIRST, SPIRITUAL STRENGTH

Spiritual Strength. I begin each day with thirty minutes to an hour of prayer. I pray and look for the divine order that God gives my life. This gives me the strength I need to tackle each day, regardless of what challenges that day might hold. It provides me with a foundation to stand upon.

Communicate. I have started looking at myself and how I communicate, not just with my former husband but with everyone. I am learning to think first and talk second. I am listening more rather than just acting on my assumptions. I am communicating better with my friends.

For example, I asked a friend for a favor and I got the standard corporate line of why she thought this might be out of reach. Instead of reacting and beginning to come up with answers on how it might be done, I just listened. Later, I said, "This is what I heard you say this morning. Am I correct?" "Yes," she said, "but. . ." and then she explained why she said that. It turns out she didn't like the person I was trying to help.

I took the time to get to the heart of the matter. Once that was communicated, we worked out a solution favorable to all.

Let Loose. I am trying to create partnerships with my associates, rather than just assume control. Part of making that happen is giving the people I work with, whether it is my administrative assistant or a contract employee, the right to tell me they disagree with my conclusions. I can only do this by being conscious all the time of my actions. When I am consciously aware of my actions, I can change.

Love. I am learning to love people without controlling them. Love does not mean control. I understand better the give and take of love. In a new relationship, I expect to give up some things. Love doesn't mean I have to give up everything, however. We can achieve a balance.

SARAH—FIRST, COMMUNICATE

Communicate. Looking back, the cliché that communication is the key holds true in my case. I was talking when I should have been listening. Even at times when I thought I was listening, I wasn't hearing. I normally did several things at once at work. So, when Marvin in his own, disjointed, way was trying to talk to me, I might be watching television or reading. "You can't be hearing me when you are doing those other things," Marvin said.

I had heard it all before, so I jumped to the conclusion that I knew what he was going to say before he said it. I never believed it would be any different than the last time.

But I have realized that if we expect or want a relationship to work, we have to do something different. So often when we talked, we were distracted by events around us, such as the phone ringing or the kid wanting attention. I know now we must have a special time and place for true communication, a time when nothing is allowed to interrupt.

I am also trying to pay attention and not only listen, but hear — hear those things that aren't always said. Lastly, I want to give more. We locked horns so often because neither of us was willing to give and compromise.

Love. I didn't understand love when we married. We started without the depth of what I would now call love. Mutual respect and friendship are so important to love. We need to be able to play, to laugh, and to talk without being judgmental of one another. To me, love means serving, being in one sense a servant. It says I truly care in actions, not just through words.

At first, I always did something special for Marvin's birthday, our anniversary, and Christmas. But, over time, I grew resentful because he wasn't reciprocating in kind. That was a red flag. If I loved him, if I really cared, then I wouldn't have cared if my actions were returned in kind.

For me now, love is caring and concern. I will never try to change anyone again. We tried to change each other. It didn't work. But genuine caring accepts that person as he or she is. That doesn't mean you are responsible for them, just that you genuinely care about what happens to them every day.

Spiritual Strength. I grew up in a religion, but I wasn't aware of my spirituality. I went to church, sang in the choir, and attended Bible studies. For a long time during my adult years, I quit church altogether. More recently, I have discovered my own spirituality, and it has filled a void I didn't even realize I had.

I have found inner peace through that sense of spirituality, a knowledge that we are all connected to a much higher power infinitely greater than ourselves. I find myself peaceful, more forgiving, more compassionate, and more aware.

I can sit on my patio now and not feel alone. I can smell the flowers, feel the breeze, listen to the insects, and be at peace. It's contagious. When you are at peace, you give an aura and others feel good around you without even knowing why.

I know that in the future, the person I love is going to have to understand his spirituality or be open to it. It will be important to our relationship.

KATE—FIRST, SPIRITUAL STRENGTH

Spiritual Strength. My journey of change began when Richard and I separated. He had asked for six months to decide what he wanted to do about our marriage. At that point, I didn't know if we had any chance to work together to make changes and save the marriage, but I felt that I had a chance for a new beginning for me, either way it went. I was unhappy with me and what I had become. In the process of carrying him, I also began carrying friends and family, and the quality of my life and relationships suffered.

The first step in my journey of change was to stop carrying not just Richard but everyone, including friends and family. Easier said than done. I didn't have the power to do it alone. I began with a prayer of forgiveness for them and myself and gave it all to God. I had always believed in God but had never put him in control. Boy, that was tough, giving up control. But when I loosened my grasp, the burden lifted, and new people and opportunities entered my life.

Let Loose. The first visible sign of the new me was letting loose of my worry and control of all the little things. It was amazing to me to see that if something on my agenda didn't happen immediately or my way, the earth didn't stop turning. I had more time to participate in life rather than control it.

I let go of the worry about financial security. Money was there when I needed it. I let go of the fear of the future, knowing that regardless of whether or not Richard came home, I could be happy.

Love. As I spent time with my daughter, now as a single parent, I sought to see the world through her eyes. She saw a world of simple pleasures and laughter and I began to laugh with her. I felt unconditional love and it filled my life.

I even achieved a new love and understanding of Richard, but I realized that I wanted a different relationship with him now. I had changed. The rules had changed. I wanted to keep this new life of hope and laughter.

As new friends entered my life, I realized that I had withdrawn over my years of marriage because of the fear of having to carry more people. Now, I enjoyed the love and support of other people and wanted to keep that in my life.

Communicate. When Richard finally announced after months of silence that he wanted to return home, I was able to communicate my new hopes for our relationship. But he had not changed in those months and wanted to return to the old rules. When I told him the old me was no longer there, thinking that my new model was an improvement for both of us, he chose to leave. I had no choice about the marriage at that point, but I continued to choose to keep working on me.

Change hasn't happened overnight and new challenges appear often. But just as often, I see miracles in my life that I never saw before and I thank God.

SOLUTIONS

These women found solutions by changing themselves in many ways. Check those that might be helpful for you.

Let Loose

- ❑ Weigh the impact of keeping control
- ❑ Change negative thought patterns
- ❑ Give up controls
- ❑ Fight the urge
- ❑ Relinquish responsibility
- ❑ Accept differences
- ❑ Tolerate alternate time frames
- ❑ Allow failure
- ❑ Seek compromise
- ❑ Don't worry about the little things

SOLUTIONS

Communicate

- ❑ Stop and breathe
- ❑ Listen, listen, hear
- ❑ Respond
- ❑ Ask questions
- ❑ Communicate feelings and expectations
- ❑ Recognize each other's needs
- ❑ Work toward consensus; agree it is OK to disagree
- ❑ Reaffirm your personal commitment
- ❑ Schedule private talk time
- ❑ Seek help instead of giving up

SOLUTIONS

Love
- ❏ Forgive
- ❏ Respect
- ❏ Try a little tenderness
- ❏ Stroke others, stroke yourself
- ❏ Be patient
- ❏ Express gratitude
- ❏ Create private memories
- ❏ Rediscover dating and romance
- ❏ Relearn to play
- ❏ Laugh a lot

SOLUTIONS

Spiritual Strength

- ❏ Trust in God
- ❏ Seek wisdom
- ❏ Connect through meditation and prayer
- ❏ Seek inner awareness
- ❏ Practice faith
- ❏ Be willing to give over
- ❏ Silently reflect
- ❏ Embrace support
- ❏ Live by The Word
- ❏ Rest in the calm

The Author

Hattie Hill, chief executive officer of the International Productivity Institute, Inc., is a business woman, entrepreneur, professional speaker, and international management consultant. Ms. Hill is also considered an expert on global leadership and diversity and women's issues and works for companies in Europe, South Africa, the United States, and the Caribbean.

Ms. Hill was one of the top "Forty Under 40" Dallas business and community leaders honored by the *Dallas Business Journal* in 1994. *Dollars and Sense Magazine* honored Ms. Hill as one of the "Best and Brightest Business Women," *Successful Meetings Magazine* named her one of their "Hot 25 Speakers," and *Mirabella Magazine* named her one of the leading "Women of the Future."

As part of her commitment to women's issues, Ms. Hill is serving as the 1996 president of the board of Leadership America, Inc., the Women's Division of the Greater Dallas Chamber of Commerce, the Advisory Boards of the Women's Resource Center of the YWCA, and the Women's Center of Dallas. Ms. Hill also serves on the Texas

Incentive and Productivity Commission, the Governing Board of Trinity Medical Center of Carrollton, Texas, the Board of the United Way of Metropolitan Dallas, The Board of Dallas' Better Business Bureau, and is serving as class president for the Society of International Business Fellows.

Ms. Hill is a columnist for *Meeting News Magazine* and is frequently quoted as an expert, most recently in *Black Enterprise Magazine* and *The Wall Street Journal*.

Order Form for Women Who Carry Their Men

Name _____

Address _____

City, State, Zip _____

Organization _____

Title _____ Phone _____

Per copy price is $18.00 plus $5.00 shipping and handling. Applicable sales tax will be applied. Call 1-800-969-6050 for quantity discounts.

VISA _____ MASTERCARD_____ AMEX _____

Acct. number _____ Exp. date _____

Signature _____

Odenwald Press
3010 LBJ Freeway, Suite 1296
Dallas, TX 75234
1-800-969-6050